The Relationship Alphabet is dedicated to all my favorite couples, including and especially, the many clients who trusted me to work out this content in real time.

Acknowledgments

It took me nearly 40 years to allow myself to be a writer. I have Rev. Frederick Buechner to blame for that. For me, the experience of reading Buechner is the experience of nodding and mulling and thinking, "I wish I'd written that." But it didn't need to be written. And so I didn't. Indeed, I didn't write a lot of things because of Frederick Buechner.

But Buechner's writing, more than most, has changed the way I think about language and life and even love. His *Whistling in the Dark: A Doubter's Dictionary* is the inspiration for working through the alphabet. In the "M" section of that book, Buechner describes an ideal marriage as one where two partners, "become more richly themselves together than the chances are either of them could have managed to become alone." This vision sustains the work I do with couples and is the thread that connects most of what I've proposed in *The Relationship Alphabet*. I suppose that means Frederick Buechner is also the reason that I do write. So, thank you sir.

Thanks to The Gottman Institute for the opportunity to contribute and for being so generous and open-handed with your content. Thanks to Drs. John and Julie Gottman and the countless therapists, researchers, and even couples who make this content so accessible and compelling. I've grown as a therapist, husband, and person by exploring and mucking about in this incredible body of knowledge through the year. Thank you for the incredible gift your work is to the world.

I owe a huge debt of gratitude to Michael Fulwiler, who was both my main source of accountability and primary cheerleader. Many, many thanks to Lindsey Thompson who brilliantly crafted the design vision for the book. And to Jo Vance, who edited my first drafts quickly, thoroughly, and graciously. Finally, I am exceedingly grateful to Anne Kennedy Brady, a powerful writer and editor, who also happens to be very good at being married. Her critical eye and curious mind brought these posts to life and will no doubt inspire many conversations for readers.

The greatest measure of my thanks belongs to my wife Rebecca who has been my primary sounding board, fact-checker, and skeptical-look-giver throughout this process. There's no one else in the world I'd rather spend my days arguing with, turning toward, and learning to love. Thanks for writing this relationship story with me.

Zach Brittle
June 2015

P.S. I would be remiss not to thank you, the reader. I appreciate that you have given me the opportunity to speak into the small corners of your relationship. More, I appreciate that you are taking the time to focus on the process of "becoming more richly yourselves together." If I can be of help to you in any way, please don't hesitate to contact me.

Foreword

from Dr. John Gottman

For the last 20 years, Julie and I have dedicated our lives to making the information from the research lab widely accessible for couples to use to strengthen their relationships. We've written books, given radio and television interviews, delivered keynote lectures, and taught workshops around the world, but none of those efforts compare to the exponential reach provided by the internet.

Our team at The Gottman Institute has been able to reach and engage with millions of couples through content shared on social media and on the Gottman Relationship Blog. Zach Brittle has been a primary contributor to the blog, and his Relationship Alphabet series has been one of our most popular with readers. It has been extremely gratifying to see so many people benefit from his work.

Zach was part of a small group of researchers I personally trained over a period of several years with the Bringing Baby Home program. As a Certified Gottman Therapist, he is a member of an exclusive cohort of expert clinicians. He has a firm grasp of the research foundation of the Gottman Method and the ability to clearly communicate it to others.

I have the greatest respect for Zach, and what he has accomplished with *The Relationship Alphabet* is simply amazing. From Arguments to Kissing to Turning, the chapters that follow bring the research to life with creativity, warmth, and humor. I am indebted to Zach for his sensitivity and honesty in writing this book. I know that his insights into the research and the questions that accompany his reflections will help couples achieve long-lasting, satisfying relationships.

John M. Gottman
June 2015

Dr. John Gottman and Zach Brittle

the relationship alphabet

A Practical Guide
to Better Connection
for Couples

#1 BESTSELLING AUTHOR

Zach Brittle

Adapted from The Gottman Relationship Blog

Zach Brittle, LMHC
zach@zachbrittle.com

ISBN-13: 978-1514891612
ISBN-10: 1514891611

www.zachbrittle.com
www.forbetter.us

Book and Cover Design by LTP Creative.

Contents

Acknowledgments I
Foreword IV

A is for Arguments 1
B is for Betrayal 7
C is for Contempt and Criticism 13
D is for Defensiveness 19
E is for Empathy 25
F is for Friendship 31
G is for Gratitude 37
H is for Humor 43
I is for Imagination 49
J is for Judgment 55
K is for Kissing 61
L is for Like and Love 67
M is for Money 73
N is for Newlyweds 79
O is for Opportunity 85
P is for Problems 91
Q is for Questions 97
R is for Repair 105
S is for Sex 111
T is for Turning 117
U is for Understanding 123
V is for Violence 129
W is for Wednesdays 137
X is for X-Rated 143
Y is for Yes 151
Z is for Zed 157

About the Author 164
About The Gottman Institute 165

A

A is for Arguments

Just for kicks, I decided to ask Google for help finding marriage and relationship words that start with "A." I got a lot of help with my Scrabble game, but not too much else. I did find one site dedicated to "marriage vocabulary." The list of "A" words included: *Acceptance*, *Admiration*, *Affection*, *Affinity*, *Allegiance*, *Appreciation*, *Approval*, and *Attentive*.

All of those words are relevant and essential to healthy relationship. They're good words. And while I think that you and your partner should *accept*, *admire*, and all those other things, I also think you should *argue*. Maybe it's just me, but I think if you're not arguing, you're probably not committed.

When engaged couples come into my office for premarital counseling, one of my first questions is, "Could you tell me about when, how, and why you argue?" If they don't or can't or won't argue, that's a major red flag. If you're in a committed relationship and you haven't yet had a big argument, please do that as soon as possible. It's important for you to understand the anatomy of your arguments so that you can uncover the patterns and themes that recur. Most importantly, it's critical for you to know that arguing is okay. It can even be productive.

It's critical for you to know that arguing is okay. It can even be productive.

When I begin therapy with a couple, I ask them to argue with one another during the first few sessions, just so we can normalize it a bit. Arguing is just part of the deal—it's one of the permissions of a committed relationship, kind of like sex. Think about it, you get to have sex with your partner *and* you get to yell at them at the top of your lungs. Can you do that with a colleague at work? (If you answered yes, maybe you should find a new job.)

John Gottman discovered that about two-thirds of all arguments are perpetual. This means that, most likely, five years from now you'll be fighting about the same thing you were fighting about five years ago. It might be her mother, or the way you put away the dishes, or his introversion—it doesn't matter. Sixty-nine percent of your problems are not going away. It's a simple, statistical fact.

Now consider this question: Is that *discouraging* or *encouraging*? Typically, when my clients find Gottman's statistic *discouraging*, it's because they know exactly what their perpetual problems are and they feel overwhelmed at the thought of spending the next thirty-five years arguing about them. But when the numbers *encourage* couples, it's usually because they realize that they're (statistically) normal. They're relieved to discover that their relationship isn't doomed just because they have the same old arguments over and over. In fact, it may be a sign that their relationship has a hope they hadn't previously imagined.

My bias is that the reality of perpetual problems is encouraging. It allows, requires, even invites, perspective about the wide range of conflicts in our relationships and the role those conflicts play. More importantly, it suggests another "A" word: *Agency*. Agency means you're not subject to the whim of the moment. On the contrary, you get to choose how you act, what you say, and when you say it, *in the midst* of each moment. It means you control the conflicts in your life, rather than the other way around.

You get to choose how you act, what you say, and when you say it, *in the midst* of each moment. It means you control the conflicts in your life, rather than the other way around.

For example, think about some of your most common points of contention with your partner. In the moment, it's easy to get caught up in the power of a single issue, but what if you took a few steps back to explore the anatomy of your arguments. How do they start? How do they escalate? How do they go off the rails? How do they end? Once you start to map out these regular arguments and understand their patterns, you'll find you can predict them, anticipate their trajectory, and perhaps even defuse them. This can seem a daunting task for those arguments that feel older than a fine wine, but give it a try. You may be surprised at the insight you gain into your relationship.

Kindness helps. It can pave the way to repair old wounds and remind you that your relationship is bigger than your argument. Humor helps. It can break the tension of the moment and provide the opportunity to connect anew. Perspective helps. It can refocus your attention, pulling back the curtain to reveal that an overwhelming impasse may in reality be a very manageable annoyance.

I'm not suggesting that some arguments aren't worth pursuing. About 31 percent of them should be addressed seriously and sometimes through therapy. It could be your anniversary. Her affair. His addiction. But for those perpetual problems—the issues that neither endanger nor desert you—make some choices. Choose kindness. Choose humor. Choose perspective. Whenever you can solve an argument, do. Whenever you can't, recognize your differences and remember that you're normal.

Whether you find it *encouraging* or *discouraging*, arguing is simply part of the sacred, beautiful, confounding reality of committed relationships. You may not get to choose what you disagree on. But you can choose what you do next.

Arguments Discussion Questions:

1. Do you remember your first fight (assuming you've had it already)? What was it about? Who won?

2. Are arguments rare or common in your relationship? How do you feel about that?

3. What do you know about your "perpetual arguments"? What do you find encouraging about Gottman's findings about perpetual conflict? What is discouraging?

4. Take a recent or common argument and apply these four questions to determine its anatomy: *How did it start? How did it escalate? How did it go off the rails? How did it end?*

5. What would you like to change about how you and your partner approach argument? What are some steps you can take to accomplish this change?

B

B is for Betrayal

There's a sentence in the introduction of Dr. John Gottman's book *What Makes Love Last?* that I find, on first glance, a little crazymaking. See if you agree: "Betrayal is the secret that lies at the heart of *every* failing relationship—it is there *even if the couple is unaware of it.*"

It just doesn't seem very Gottman-esque. This sentence implies that (a) there is a single secret and (b) it applies in 100 percent of failing relationships. Dr. Gottman's body of research always seems to include options—there are *seven* principles, *four* horsemen, *two* kinds of marital conflict. And nothing is 100 percent—divorce is predicted with 91 percent accuracy, 35 percent of husbands are emotionally intelligent, and 70 percent of couples that have sex are unhappy with the frequency or quality of the sex. Additionally, it implies that relationship failure isn't caused by a deficit in communication, compatibility, or chemistry—three of the most popular relationship clichés—but rather the presence of betrayal, the one thing you swore you'd never tolerate.

According to Dr. Gottman, however, if your relationship is struggling, you have indeed tolerated—or perhaps perpetrated—betrayal. "Hold your horses," you might say (but probably not, because nobody says that anymore). "I've never had an affair. My partner has never had an affair. How can you say betrayal is the cause of our relationship troubles?" It's a fair question. It's easy to lump "betrayal" and "infidelity" into the same bucket. Indeed, all affairs, even emotional ones, require a duplicity that tears at the fabric of commitment. But the affair is never the beginning of the betrayal. It's simply one possible outcome.

I'll be the first to admit that infidelity is the juiciest and most dramatic of betrayals—that's why we love to absorb *The Good Wife* and *Scandal* and *Homeland* and *Grey's Anatomy* and even *Betrayal* from the comfort of our living rooms. But it's neither the most common nor the most dangerous form of betrayal. More damaging are the everyday betrayals that sneak up on you. The ones that pile up over time as you and your partner continually ask and answer the question,"Can I trust you?"

Can I trust you to pick up the milk? To listen to my feelings? To not get drunk at that party? To respect my time? To focus on our kids instead of the television? To choose me? For better *and* for worse? Again? And again?

Most of you are convinced that your spouse would never cheat on you. But are you as certain that he will genuinely care about your anxieties and fears? That she will graciously hear you confess your suspicion that you may be a fraud? That he will still think you're beautiful when you no longer look like the pretty young thing he married way back when? When the "No"s pile up, you start to look for "Yes" in other places. That's when alternative outcomes avail themselves. The extra glass of wine you pour after the first extra glass. The stay-at-home dad with the great smile. Your mother's patient, listening ear. Opportunities for full blown betrayal are everywhere.

When the "No"s pile up, you start to look for "Yes" in other places.

Seems pretty grim, but I say hold your horses. There's good news. There may be a single secret to failing relationships, but there's also a simple solution. It goes like this:

"Can I trust you?"

"*Yes.*"

The trick is learning how to get to Yes. It's important to suspend for now the notion that one of you is the betrayer and the other is the betrayed. You are both responsible, and you both need to figure out how to get to Yes.

I'll give you a hint. The way to Yes is through a bonus B-word right at the heart of Gottman's body of research: Bids. A bid is simply the expression of a need for connection. Maybe you need to feel supported in a new business endeavor. Maybe your partner needs to talk through a frustrating experience. Maybe you want to share a funny story. In any case, you are responsible for making bids toward your partner rather than the pretty lady at the gym. You are also responsible for turning toward your partner's bids rather than burying your nose in your phone. Bids aren't complicated—just pay attention. Be present. Show him that you are trustworthy by listening to what he says, answering his question, laughing at his joke (even the one you heard before). Prove that you trust her by asking her advice, playing with her, complimenting her taste.

You are also responsible for turning toward your partner's bids rather than burying your nose in your phone.

You *can* ward off those sneaky, small, everyday betrayals—the key is to build a big pile of Yes. Concentrate first on "Yes, I am trustworthy," and lean into "Yes, I trust you." Betrayal may be the root cause of every troubled relationship, but Yes is at the heart of every thriving one. Trust me.

Betrayal Discussion Questions:

1. How do you feel when you read Gottman's "crazymaking" sentence in the first paragraph? Do you agree with him?
2. How do you make bids toward your partner? How are those bids received?
3. What are some ways betrayal could creep (or has creeped) into your own relationship? What can you do to stop it?
4. Identify what "alternative outcomes" exist in your world. How might trust in and from your partner help you steer clear of those options?
5. In what ways is it easy to trust your partner? In what areas is it more difficult? In what ways do you think it's easy or difficult for your partner to trust you? What would it look like to commit to fostering greater trust in each other?

C

C is for Contempt and Criticism

A cornerstone of Dr. John Gottman's approach to predicting relationship success is what he calls "The Four Horsemen of the Apocalypse." He suggests that there are four behaviors that poison our relationships and sabotage our goal of deeper intimacy. Contempt and criticism are the first two "horsemen"—at least alphabetically.

In case you're unfamiliar with Gottman's biblical allusion, allow me to explain. The Four Horsemen of the Apocalypse is a reference to the book of Revelation, the last book of the New Testament. In the sixth chapter, four horses and riders appear to signal the end of the world as we know it. The white horse is first, and his rider emerges "as a conqueror bent on conquest" (Rev 6:2 NIV). He is soon followed by a fiery red horse, whose rider bears a large sword and the "power to take peace from the earth and make men slay each other" (Rev 6:4 NIV).

There are two more horsemen (black and pale) but for now, let's focus on the first two. These messengers of conquest and violence are powerful symbols of their relationship twins: contempt and criticism. When contempt and criticism are allowed to run free in your relationship, chaos ensues and destruction is imminent. But they can be sneaky. No one just *decides* one day to show contempt to their partner. No one wakes up suddenly determined to criticize the person they love. So how can you tell if you've fallen victim to these behaviors? And how can you break the habit?

When contempt and criticism are allowed to run free in your relationship, chaos ensues and destruction is imminent.

Contempt as Conquest

Gottman has called contempt the greatest predictor of divorce. For years, however, I misunderstood the word. I used to think contempt was "I hate you." Kind of the way the Hatfields feel about the McCoys. Or the way my daughters feel about each other these days. You want this, I want that. We can't agree, so let's not even try. It's easier to fight than to reconcile anyway. In short, I viewed contempt as something blatant—and certainly harmful—but simple.

But contempt isn't "I hate you." It's something much worse—something insidious and gross. Contempt is "I'm better than you." If betrayal is a question of trust, then contempt is a question of respect. Contempt says,

"I don't respect you. In fact, I'm going to actively disrespect you." Name-calling is a dead giveaway, but contempt can also be more subtle, like correcting your partner's grammar at a dinner party, throwing out a "funny" sarcastic comment that dismisses their point of view, or even eye-rolling. However it manifests, the contemptuous partner is "bent on conquest," seeking to ensure the other knows who is superior. I've seen this a lot in religious and politically conservative relationships where the woman, or at least her role, is assumed to be "less than." But I've seen plenty of relationships where the woman has mastered contempt as well. (Their husbands are usually pretty great at stonewalling—another apocalyptic Horseman.)

So what can you do? Gottman suggests nurturing fondness and admiration for your partner as the antidote for contempt, but I wonder if that's enough. I suspect that, in most cases of contempt, the real target is the self. Yes, nurturing fondness for your partner is critical, but it's at least equally important to become aware of your own capacity for contempt. Only then can you can begin working on the problem at its root.

Criticism as Violence

Gottman's research suggests that criticism may be the least destructive horseman, but it is violent nonetheless. Criticism is an assault against your partner and has "the power to take peace" from your relationship. It is designed to slay the other.

Criticism is often packaged in "you always" or "you never" statements. The implication is that the offending partner hasn't simply *offended*, but actually *is* offensive. In other words, criticism is aimed at a person's character rather than their behavior. Not surprisingly, this kind of attack often triggers defensiveness and leads to a cycle of conflict that is hard to escape.

Gottman suggests replacing criticism with "I statements," the most tried and-true of marriage counseling clichés. And in fact, "I statements" do help direct you toward complaining about the behavior without blaming the person. I want to stress, however, that this is more than a skill. It's a state of mind. "You always" and "you never" defer responsibility to the partner, but *you* are responsible. You are. Your criticism is a wish disguised—it's a negative expression of a real need.

So, what if you took responsibility for what you really desire for the relationship? What if you owned the wish and committed to articulating it as a positive hope? It could be as simple as starting your sentences with "I wish" instead of "you never." But as with contempt, it requires a good, hard introspective look. In this case, you must examine your own inclination toward violence as you work to change your behavior from the inside out.

Getting What You Want

I'll admit, it's tempting. Who doesn't want to feel strong and powerful? Who doesn't want to be right? And in a relationship fraught with conflict, wielding contempt and criticism can seem like a great way to seize a measure of control. But whenever I encounter any of Gottman's Four Horsemen with clients, I circle back to the same question: *Does this behavior help you get what you want?* The answer is always the same: *No*. So, then, if there's no other reason to avoid contempt and criticism, consider the fact that they simply don't work. Both may make you feel good for a moment, but disrespecting or belittling your partner will *never* yield the response—or more importantly, the change—you are seeking.

So, "hold your horses." Don't allow contempt and criticism to run free. Rein them in and replace them with compassion for yourself and for your partner. That way, you can dream *together* about how to get what you really want from your relationship.

Contempt and Criticism Discussion Questions:

1. Why do you think Gottman compares contempt and criticism to a biblical image of the world's destruction?

2. Why do you think research discovered criticism to be "least destructive horseman" and contempt to be "the greatest predictor of divorce"? Do you agree?

3. What are some ways contempt and criticism have manifested in your relationships—past and/or present? How were/are the relationships affected?

4. What might your capacity for contempt say about your own needs, fears, or dreams? What about your inclination toward violence and criticism? Why is it important to examine these things as you try to change your behavior?

5. Discuss with your partner what you both want from your relationship. How would contempt and criticism keep you from reaching your relationship dreams? What kind of checks and balances can you put in place to rein in these two horsemen.

D

D is for Defensiveness

The bride of my youth is delighted that I'm writing about defensiveness. She's been chuckling under her breath at me all week. "How's your chapter coming?" she asks. "I'm not exactly sure what to write," I say. "Just write about yourself," she teases. You see, I really get defensiveness. Which is to say, I get defensive. Often.

Defensiveness, defined as "any attempt to defend oneself from perceived attack," is the third of Dr. Gottman's Four Horsemen of the Apocalypse (the other three being Criticism, Contempt, and Stonewalling). This particularly sneaky Horseman manifests itself primarily in three ways: righteous indignation, counterattack, and whining. Over the years, I've become something of an expert in all three.

One Saturday morning not long ago, we went to Costco to stock up for the week. When we got home, the family scattered. The kids were folding some laundry. My wife was tying up some loose ends around the house. I put the groceries away. Soup in the pantry. Milk in the fridge. Chicken in the freezer. When the family later decided that we would have the chicken for dinner, my wife was dismayed to discover it would need some serious defrosting. She smirked at me as she tossed our rock-solid dinner into the microwave. "Ugh," she said, "you're *always* in such a hurry to put stuff in the freezer!" As a grown adult, I like to think such charming teasing, however ridiculous, doesn't affect me. Instead, I said, "Don't you mean, 'Thanks for shopping for, buying, carrying, and putting away all the groceries?'" Which is also ridiculous, but slightly less charming.

I'm generally pretty sure that my wife is not trying to attack me, yet even a good-natured ribbing about chicken in the freezer triggers something defensive in me.

My response, in case you couldn't tell, was a classic case of righteous indignation. Righteous indignation is a fancy way to say getting pissy in response to a perceived attack, rather than trusting that your partner isn't actually trying to tear you down. I'm generally pretty sure that my wife is not trying to attack me, yet even a good-natured ribbing about chicken in the freezer triggers something defensive in me. My indignant responses are truly unconscious. My *impulse* is to immediately refute or rebut whatever is coming my way, and I respond impulsively, rather than thoughtfully.

As fun as righteous indignation is, my favorite way to get defensive is to counterattack. Counterattack is one step beyond indignation. It's an escalation of conflict through scorekeeping. Whenever I feel attacked, I immediately start planning my retaliation. Again, it's an impulse. I cannot tell you the number of times this has happened: An argument starts, possibly over frozen chicken. I *feel* attacked, so I counterattack. She says, "Don't get defensive." I get more defensive. I yell. She yells. I yell louder. She cries. I win. But in fact, we both lose. In the end, we have no idea what we were actually arguing about and dinner is still frozen.

A third manifestation of defensiveness is acting like the innocent victim, often by whining. This is the sneakiest one. I believe that most people who default to victimization don't realize they're doing it, or if they do, they've colored their whining as sacrifice. My wife calls it "swinging the door" when I do it. I totally abandon my position in the hopes that she will feel terrible and give me what I want. "Okay fine. I promise I will never, ever put the chicken in the freezer before I get permission from you." This isn't generous sacrifice or thoughtful compromise – this is passive aggression designed to shut down communication and make the other person feel awful. It's childish and destructive and very easy to do.

I see this kind of unconscious victimization all the time with my clients. He may express a concern, legitimate or otherwise. Then she will explain, often through tears, why his concern isn't her fault. Just as often, she'll end up explaining why *everything* is probably her fault. Suddenly, her reaction distracts from the concern itself, and communication breaks down. But she's not being manipulative. Once again, it's an impulse, in this case to make sure that someone else can't shame us more than we can shame ourselves.

Defensiveness is a wicked game. But it's winnable. If betrayal is about the question of trust and contempt is about the question of respect, then defensiveness is about the question of responsibility. That's the antidote: accepting responsibility for your role in the issue. Think about the word 'responsibility' for a second.

Response. Ability.

You have that. You are not subject to the whims of your impulses. You have the ability to respond with patience, grace, humility, and even strength. The key is to understand the difference between a *perceived attack* and an actual one. It's also a good idea to be aware of your and your partner's triggers, as you work toward addressing conflict in a responsible manner. (Note to my bride: Telling me not to get defensive triggers my defensiveness.)

The key is to understand the difference between a *perceived attack* and an actual one.

Responsibility takes courage. It's safer to counterattack. It feels better to shoot back a snarky, indignant comment. It's easier to play the victim. But all of these responses are barriers to a healthy relationship. Next time you feel attacked, identify what it is that set you off and recognize that you're not controlled by your impulses. Then take a risk. *Choose* a response that will open communication and bolster your relationship, rather than protect your pride. After all, it's only chicken.

Defensiveness Discussion Questions:

1. How can the three types of defensiveness each damage communication in a relationship?
2. Think about a time you reacted defensively. How did your defensiveness manifest itself? Can you identify a trigger in the situation?
3. Do you agree that defensiveness is about the question of responsibility? Why or why not?
4. What topics frequently get your defenses up? Why do you think that is?
5. If the impulse to defend is about protection, then choosing not to be defensive is dangerous. Why would such danger improve a relationship? Discuss the risks and rewards with your partner.

E

E is for Empathy

Let's review the Relationship Alphabet so far:

A is for Arguing
B is for Betrayal
C is for Contempt and Criticism
D is for Defensiveness

Pretty grim, right? Not what you signed up for when you got married? Actually, you might have. If you had a wedding you probably stood up in front of a bunch of people and promised something like "for better or for worse." A through D represents the best of the worst. But it gets better. Because E is for Empathy.

I've been obsessed with empathy for a while now, and I'm not alone. There's a pretty vibrant debate these days about whether empathy is a necessary leadership quality. Many high-profile (and high-profit) companies are thriving despite their leaders' lack of "people skills," but psychologist Daniel Goleman cites empathy as the cornerstone of emotional intelligence, an essential quality for the successful leadership. In the medical field, one recent study found that doctors who are more empathetic generally have patients with better outcomes.[1] But this research only confirms what we intuitively know. After all, the term "bedside manner" was coined long before that study.

CEOs have to have it. Doctors have to have it. Presumably anyone who wants to obey the Golden Rule or walk a mile in somebody else's shoes has to have it. *But what is it?*

Dr. Gottman describes empathy as mirroring a partner's feelings in a way that lets them know their feelings are understood and shared.

Empathy is generally understood as the capacity to identify and share someone else's emotions and experiences. Dr. Gottman describes empathy as mirroring a partner's feelings in a way that lets them know their feelings are understood and shared. He cites it as the key to attunement with your partner as well as essential to the "emotion coaching" style of parenting. As a husband and a father, I cling to Gottman's wisdom on empathy—after all, he's earned his stripes over forty years of research. But if I'm honest, my absolute favorite perspective on the concept comes from a little boy.

One of my favorite books of all time is Orson Scott Card's *Ender's Game*. On the surface, it's your typical

---

1. Brandy King, "How Does Physician Empathy Affect Patient Outcomes?" http://humanism-in-medicine/, (July 3, 2013).

story of intergalactic warfare with a race of alien bugs. But it's also a brilliant case study in empathy as demonstrated through the character of Ender Wiggin, a young boy with an unusual aptitude for battle strategy as well as an enormous capacity for compassion. Reflecting on the central conflict of the novel, Ender says:

> *In the moment when I truly understand my enemy, understand him well enough to defeat him, then in that very moment I also love him. I think it's impossible to really understand somebody, what they want, what they believe, and not love them the way they love themselves.*[2]

There's quite a bit going on here. Ender begins with an insight into conflict, and the reader expects to learn how he will achieve victory over his enemy. Victory, however, isn't the goal. At least it's not the *only* goal. Ender is chasing understanding, and that understanding leads to love. To have empathy is to understand somebody fully—what they want, what they believe. And not just in the moment, but in general.

As a therapist, my goal is to help couples understand this concept. Often, they come into my office thinking of one another as the enemy. They're entrenched in patterns of argument, betrayal, contempt, criticism and defensiveness, and they have a hard time achieving or even seeking understanding. I remind them that the enemy

2. Orson Scott Card, Ender's Game (New York: Tor, 1991), 168.

mindset doesn't help them get what they want—trust, respect, understanding, intimacy. Instead, these things are built through a commitment to hear not only the complaint but also the dream embedded in the conflict. You're arguing about the groceries, but what does your partner truly *want*? To be heard? To be appreciated? This is hard work. It may require you to be a master tactician, strategically deploying conflict management skills. More often it requires you to shift your mindset from "enemy" to "partner" in the battle for your relationship.

You're arguing about the groceries, but what does your partner truly *want*? To be heard? To be appreciated?

You may be a CEO or a doctor. Maybe you're a husband or a wife or a parent. It's possible you're a therapist. You are most definitely a person, and I'll bet you want to be in safe, interesting, life-giving relationships. I urge you to become obsessed with empathy. Once you fully commit to understanding another person, I'd be surprised if you don't start to love them, as one little boy observed, in the same way they love themselves.

Empathy Discussion Questions:

1. Why might empathy be a critical character trait in medical and business professionals?
2. Do you agree that empathy is the key to attunement with your partner? Why or why not?
3. Can you identify moments in which you felt empathy for your partner? What about when you felt empathy *from* them? How was your relationship impacted?
4. Have there been times when you viewed your partner as an "enemy"? How might empathy have helped change your perspective?
5. Commit to choosing empathy in your relationships for one month. How do you think this will manifest itself? With whom, or in what situations, might this be most difficult? Keep track of your feelings throughout the month and note what, if anything, changes.

F

F is for Friendship

I was at a job interview a while back when the interviewer asked me, "What three words would your best friend use to describe you?" I like the question, but it took me a moment to respond. It wasn't because I couldn't find the words. It was because I couldn't decide who my best friend was. Eventually I said, "I think my wife would describe me as tall, dark, and handsome." I expected a laugh but my interviewer just looked at me. Baffled and a little incredulous, he said, "Your wife is your best friend?"

It sounds odd–spouses as friends, or certainly as *best* friends. Aren't spouses and friends categorically different? I would argue that they shouldn't be. In fact, deep friendship is the foundational level of Dr. Gottman's Sound Relationship House Theory of happy couples. It is the root of commitment and trust. And just as importantly, it forms the basis for intimacy and satisfying sex. In *The Seven Principles for Making Marriage Work*, Dr. Gottman says that couples with deep friendships have:

> *...mutual respect and enjoyment of each other's company. They tend to know each other intimately – they are well versed in each other's likes, dislikes, personality quirks, hopes and dreams. They have an abiding regard for each other and express this fondness not just in the big ways but in little ways day in and day out.*

Gottman's definition includes one of my favorite words: Regard. I use it all the time when counseling couples, especially in early sessions. When couples have even a basic regard for one another, there is hope for therapy. Gottman Method Couples Therapy (GMCT) helps couples build friendships through a variety of interventions designed to help them develop mutual respect and enjoyment, but those interventions are often fruitless without regard.

When couples have even a basic regard for one another, there is hope for therapy.

So, how do you foster regard? I think it begins by developing two simple skills: asking questions and telling stories.

First, learn to ask profound questions. One of my favorite leadership mentors, Bobb Biehl is a collector of questions with a powerful philosophy: *If you ask profound questions, you get profound answers; if you ask shallow questions, you get shallow answers; and if you ask no questions, you get no answers at all.*[1] Any question is better than no question, but profound questions deliver the greatest rewards. One of the core interventions of GMCT is learning to ask open-ended (i.e. profound) questions, because they lead to a rich understanding of your partner's inner world–*Love Maps* in the Gottman vernacular. Detailed Love Maps are an essential step toward deep friendships for couples.

Like most things, it takes practice. It's much easier to ask, "Did you have a good day at work?" than "How did you feel about your presentation today?" Or even, "Are you upset?" rather than "You seem upset – what's going on?" Profound questions can be difficult not only because shallow questions often become a habit, but also because it's harder to predict the response. You have to be prepared for longer answers, or painful answers, or confusing answers. Or fascinating, exciting, revealing answers. But if your goal is friendship and intimacy, you'll give it a shot, and you'll find it makes the next skill a little easier.

The second skill that helps foster regard is telling stories. We all know somebody who is a great storyteller—someone who can hold the attention of any room, any time, anywhere. Whenever I hang out with that guy, I end up feeling like I'm a "bad storyteller." But that's simply not true. I've got great stories, and so do you, but many of us have never even told our own

1. Bobb Biehl, Asking Profound Questions http://www.bobbbiehl.com, (May 17, 2014).

stories. If you're in that group, give it a try! Start with "I was born in..." and just keep going. What comes out of your mouth may surprise you, and if your listener is curious and caring, the opportunity for discovery is boundless. Every story is important. Your family story. Your first kiss story. Your broken leg story. They all hold insights into *you* and how you think about relationships.

Friends tend to "glorify the struggle," discussing how hard times have shaped and strengthened their relationship.

As a couple you should also tell your collective story. Stories have the power to transform relationships because they provide context for the rough spots and remind us that there is something bigger than the struggle. Whenever a new couple comes in, one of the first things I do is ask for their whole story. It's invariably filled with ups and downs, laughter and tears. And while the facts are important, *how* a couple tells their story is just as critical because it reveals the health of their friendship. Friends tend to "glorify the struggle," discussing how hard times have shaped and strengthened their relationship. Couples whose friendship is broken focus more on the difficulties of the struggle itself. In order to build or rebuild regard, it's important to learn to identify perseverance, connection, and joy within the struggles of your story.

So, ask questions. Tell stories. Indulge curiosity and discovery. Create context for exploring each other's likes, dislikes, personality quirks, hopes, and dreams. Focusing on your friendship and cultivating regard is the best thing you can do for your relationship as a whole. And the best part? It's not terribly complicated. Maybe start by asking, "What three words would you use to describe me?"

Friendship Discussion Questions:

1. Do find it strange to describe your spouse as your friend? Why or why not?
2. What three words would you use to describe your partner? How do you think your partner would describe you?
3. How can asking profound questions make storytelling easier?
4. If you haven't already, try sharing your own story with your partner. What pieces of your own story might inform how you approach relationships?
5. Write down your story as a couple, and ask your partner to do the same. Compare your stories and notice similarities and differences. How do you each portray the struggle?

G

G is for Gratitude

If I had to guess, I'd say that few of us have spent much time really thinking about gratitude. Sure, we write thank you notes now and again, we reflexively say thank you to our servers and bartenders (as well we should), and we've been known to utter a quick "thank God" when we find our lost wallet. And who hasn't spent at least one Thanksgiving taking turns announcing "what we're thankful for" before the turkey gets carved? But I would argue that this often brushed-over practice deserves a little more attention. I think gratitude can change the current of our relationships.

And I'm not alone. Consider Brother David Steindle-Rast, a Benedictine monk, author, and prolific lecturer, who theorizes that if you want to be happy, be grateful. In a TED Talk from 2013, Steindle-Rast gently argues that grateful living comes from an awareness that "every moment is a given moment."[1] Therefore, if every moment is a gift, then every moment is worthy of

1. David Steindle-Rast, "Want to be happy? Be grateful," http://ted.com (June 2013).

gratitude, and an abundance of gratitude translates into less fear and violence in the world. More contentment. Less scarcity.

Maybe that's too mystical for you. Maybe you're more inclined toward facts than theories. Consider that contemporary research is starting to expand the science and practice of gratitude. Recent studies have shown that people who consistently practice gratitude have stronger immune systems and lower blood pressure. They have higher levels of positive emotions like joy, optimism, and happiness. They're more likely to "pay it forward" with generosity and compassion.

If every moment is a gift, then every moment is worthy of gratitude, and an abundance of gratitude translates into less fear and violence in the world.

Still not convinced? Maybe you're more inspired by obedience. The Apostle Paul implores us to "give thanks in all circumstances." (1 Thess. 5:18 NIV) Jesus likes that. Or maybe you love etiquette, and you definitely mailed every thank-you note before your first anniversary. Or, does your heart bleed for mid-90's pop music? The band Geggy Tah celebrated gratitude in their one hit "Whoever You Are:" *All I wanna do is to thank you / Even though I don't know who you are / You let me change lanes / While I was driving in my car.*

So, what does this have to do with your relationships? Everything.

Gratitude *is* relational. It shifts our focus from ourselves to one another, which is critical because, guess what? We're all narcissists. We're all looking out for our own best interests the vast majority of the time. And while that may be great for our stock portfolio, it doesn't work too well in a relationship. Gratitude invites us—actually *requires* us—to abandon our narcissism and remember that we are not alone. That reminder in itself is a gift, because the very fact that you are not alone means that you can experience empathy, intimacy, and love. And that's worth being grateful for! So you see, the more you express gratitude, the more reasons exist to be grateful.

Gratitude is the secret that could put therapists out of a job: if couples would shift away from defensiveness and toward gratitude on their own, they wouldn't need to seek counseling. It's certainly a muscle that requires exercise, but the thing about gratitude is that it's so simple to get started. All you have to do is say "Thank you for ______." It may feel difficult or forced to fill in the blank at first. But if you make it a habit, it becomes just that. Here's a trick: Set an alarm on your phone (or your watch or whatever), and when it goes off, send a quick note of thanks to your partner. It can be for something big or something tiny, something silly or something very serious. It can be for something for which they "already know" you're thankful (they may not). Maybe do it a couple days in a row. See how long it takes them to notice.

They will notice. Everybody likes to be thanked. No

one in the history of ever has said, "Please don't thank me, it makes me feel terrible." Being appreciated feels great. It makes us feel uniquely known, which increases our sense of worth and value. And it's contagious. I guarantee you that if you work gratitude into your relationship – even secretly – it will come back to you. Even if it's not the way you expect, you'll feel happier and healthier.

Gratitude is a rising tide that lifts all boats in the relationship.

Gratitude is a rising tide that lifts all boats in the relationship. It's a simple, powerful way to strengthen the friendship aspect of your overall relationship. It accelerates the shift to the positive perspective and leads quite naturally to fueling fondness and admiration for one other. So commit to thinking more deeply about gratitude and injecting it into your relationships. Start small. Set that alarm. Write a note. Give thanks before dinner, if only to begin your meal with something besides your hunger. I promise you'll be surprised by the changes even a narcissist like you or me can bring about through simple acts of appreciation.

Gratitude Discussion Questions:

1. Do you agree with Brother David Steindle-Rast's theory that every moment is a gift, and therefore deserves gratitude? Why or why not?
2. Why do you think studies show higher rates of positive emotions and lower blood pressure in people who regularly express gratitude?
3. Think of a time someone expressed appreciation for something you did or said. What feelings are connected with that memory?
4. Make a list of five things you are grateful for in your partner. Have you told them you're grateful for these things? Why or why not?
5. What are some ways you and your partner could inject gratitude into your relationship so that it becomes a habit? How does it feel to think about starting this process?

H

H is for Humor

When I was in ninth grade, I saw *Who Framed Roger Rabbit* six times in the movie theater. I have probably watched it at least once a year since then. It is my favorite movie of all time. I am not kidding.

First of all, Bob Hoskins is a genius. He and his thick British accent seamlessly disappear into the character of Eddie Valiant, an alcoholic private investigator in depression-era Hollywood. On top of that, he spends half the movie acting opposite a cartoon rabbit. But the real reason it's my favorite movie is that cartoon rabbit. Roger is a scrawny, precocious, hilariously odd yet lovable character, and not terribly unlike ninth grade me.

Roger's wife, Jessica, is a beautiful, sophisticated, classic noir femme fatale, complete with smoky voice and endless curves. (She's not bad, she's just drawn that way.) Roger is crazy in love with her. And even though Jessica is apparently way out of Roger's league, she's crazy in love with him, too. Eddie can't understand it, so he asks her, with more than a little suspicion, "What do you see in that guy anyway?" Jessica responds simply:

"He makes me laugh."

All of a sudden, ninth grade me had hope. Is it possible that a good sense of humor is enough to get—and keep—the girl? Grown-up me happens to think it is.

Humor has been woven into our relational DNA since the earliest of days. Reuters claims that the world's oldest recorded joke can be traced to 1900 BC (yep, it's toilet humor). Even Aristotle believed laughter is what separates us from the beasts, and that a baby does not have a soul until the moment it laughs—usually around day forty. So if laughter is what makes us human, then humor is critical to relationships as a necessary tie that binds us to one another.

An artfully deployed inside joke can shift the focus away from your fixed position and toward your shared history.

Monty Python's John Cleese, who understands humor more than most, has said, "a wonderful thing about true laughter is that it just destroys any kind of system of dividing people."[1] This is especially true in our most personal relationships. During the course of his research Dr. Gottman was able to organize couples into two categories: *masters* and *disasters*. The disasters were prone to "systems of dividing," and specifically the Four Horsemen of the Apocalypse: contempt, criticism,

1. Nathan Rabin, "John Cleese," http://www.avclub.com (Feb 5, 2008).

defensiveness and stonewalling. The masters, on the other hand, developed effective strategies for dismantling those systems. Dr. Gottman calls these strategies *repair attempts.*

We'll go deeper into the concept of repair in a later chapter, but for now just know that, according to Dr. Gottman, repair attempts are "any statement or action that prevents negativity from escalating out of control." He calls repair attempts are the "secret weapon of emotionally intelligent couples." Masters repair early and often using a variety of strategies—including humor.

Humor is a powerful repair technique. It can lower the tension level of an argument, destroy the division between you and your partner, and remind both of you that you're human and imperfect. An artfully deployed inside joke can shift the focus away from your fixed position and toward your shared history. It's an emotional repair without an emotional conversation.

It's important to note, however, that humor can also backfire. If humor is your *only* strategy, you risk diluting its power, and it should always be balanced with sincerity. That way, you're working to repair conflict rather than ignore an issue. Also, any humor that expresses criticism or contempt or belittles the other's point of view (like sarcasm) will not serve to repair the relationship, but will actually deepen the conflict.

Remember that repair attempts are the "secret weapon" of emotionally intelligent couples. Humor is the *most* secret because it's *your* secret. As you and your partner build your friendship and collect experiences, keep an eye out for comedy. Be open to the ridiculous, the surprising, the awkward. Watch Monty Python sketches. Buy a joke book if you have to. Build up a storehouse of shared humor that will bolster your relationship in moments of conflict and beyond.

As you and your partner build your friendship and collect experiences, keep an eye out for comedy.

In *Who Framed Roger Rabbit*, Eddie literally uses humor to save Roger and Jessica's lives. While it's unlikely that any of you will be terrorized by a pack of weasels armed with toxic Dip, the symbolism is clear. Relationships are in constant danger of toxic systems. Take it from ninth grade me: a strong sense of humor is a powerful weapon.

Humor Discussion Questions:

1. What movies, shows, or books make you laugh? What makes your partner laugh?
2. Why do you think laughter breaks down systems of dividing people?
3. Have you ever tried using humor to repair a conflict? If so, what happened? If not, what might that look like?
4. Can you remember a time when sarcasm was used in the context of a conflict? What happened? How might sincere humor have looked different?
5. What inside jokes have you cultivated as a couple? Why do you think it important to have secret, shared humor with your partner? How can you make yourself open to filling your storehouse with more?

I

I is for Imagination

I fully intended this chapter to be about *Integrity*. The word gets thrown around a lot in conversations about good behavior, but I feel like that's too preachy. Instead, I prefer to think of integrity the same way architects do: to mean whole, undivided, and sound in construction.

This would have been an easy direction to take, given that the Gottman Method features its own architectural metaphor in the Sound Relationship House[1] (SRH). The SRH derives its integrity from the twin pillars of trust and commitment. Without these, Dr. Gottman suggests, his "Seven Principles for Making Marriage Work" won't work. I would have argued that it's just as important for you to have personal integrity–a sound internal construction–as it is to have relationship integrity. But that started to sound too preachy.

So I turned my attention toward *Intent*. I love intent! Intentionality is essential to a healthy relationship

1. I'll refer to the Sound Relationship House (SRH) throughout the book, so I've included it at the back of the book for you to examine at your discretion.

because it proves that you aren't interested in settling for the status quo—you're willing to work for greater intimacy and friendship. When intentionality fades, couples drift into that "ships in the night" stage. So when couples tell me they feel more like roommates than lovers (and I hear that often) I tell them to do something together. Anything. It doesn't have to be therapy, but it helps. Maybe just pick up the *Seven Principles* book and try a few of the exercises. It doesn't have to be a standing date night, but that helps. You could simply learn a new board game together. Commit to Spaghetti Sunday or Wine Wednesday or "Monday is Funday." Pick a show to binge watch together. It almost doesn't matter what you do, just do it on purpose.

Thing is, that's about all I have to say. I don't need 750 words to talk about Intent. So, I considered writing about *Infidelity*, but then I'd need a lot more than 750 words. *Intercourse*. That's a stretch. *Individuation*. Snore. *Ignorance*. It's bliss. Check. *In-laws*. Another time. Ultimately, I was stuck for the right word heading into a family vacation to Disney World.

And then it hit me. Have you ever considered the power of *Imagination*?

Walt Disney did. And he discovered that power was limitless. The Disney parks are a testament to idea that there is no such thing as no such thing. Talking mouse? Sure. Sleeping Beauty's castle in southern California? Why not? Build a Walt Disney *World* in central Florida? You bet! Entire theses have been written about the Disney philosophy and business model, but I won't attempt to explore those here. I'll just say that wandering around Walt Disney World, I was constantly in awe of the power of imagination. Often enough it was some detail or presentation at the parks themselves. Just as often it was the astonishment on my daughter's face or the laughter in her voice. For just a few days we forgot that we were real people living in a real world. We were Treasured Guests at the Happiest Place on Earth.

For just a few days we forgot that we were real people living in a real world.

I am, of course, a champion of trust and commitment in a marriage, and I believe they are critical to the integrity of a Sound Relationship house. That said, I think at least two other pillars are required. The first is *Hope*, which I won't expand here except to say that a couple with even a grain of hope has a chance. The other is *Imagination*.

I believe, as Dr. Gottman suggests, that marriage is a creative endeavor. Whenever two people come together in a relationship, they are creating a brand new culture. Genesis, the first book of the Bible, says that in a marriage, two become one. That process certainly requires some creative math. The top floor of the SRH invites couples to create shared meaning. And all creative endeavors require imagination.

In a marriage, imagination is a willingness to believe that your relationship can be different from your parents', your friends', or even from your own relationship six years ago. Or six months ago. For engaged couples, it's the active dreaming about what their relationship will become on the other side of the altar. For couples in distress, it's a chosen conviction (or, *Hope*) that the relationship can be better than it ever was. For you, it might simply be "Monday is Funday."

You have to be willing to expand your thinking and to risk believing there is no such thing as no such thing.

In any case, you have to be willing to expand your thinking and to risk believing there is no such thing as no such thing. Your marriage can have integrity and intention through trust, commitment, hope, and imagination. Start today by planning that one thing you never thought you could, or would. Find a therapist. Go to a Magic Kingdom. Do something. *Anything*. Imagine the possibilities.

Imagination Discussion Questions:

1. Do you agree that marriage is a creative endeavor? Why or why not?
2. How have you and your partner been creative in your relationship? Can you see the benefits of taking creative risks together?
3. How are "Intention" and "Imagination" connected? How do you think they both impact "Integrity"?
4. Think about your relationship one year from today. What do you want it to look like? How do you think you could get there? What are your partner's dreams?
5. Make a list of things you "never thought you could, or would" plan. What stops you from planning these things? Is there anything you can commit to right now? If you were to commit to that one thing, how might your relationship benefit?

J

J is for Judgment

J is an eight-point letter in Scrabble®. Only Q and Z are worth more. Turns out there simply aren't a lot of words that start with J. This fact is especially true in the area of relationships—a fact I discovered when I sat down to write this chapter. So, as I often do when I'm stuck, I turned to the back in one of the Gottman books and searched the index for inspiration. I found "jealousy" and "Jews, Orthodox," and whole lot of last names, but finally, there at the end of the J column, the perfect topic was just waiting for me. Judgment.

Surprised? I decided on judgment mostly because "judgment" and "judging" and "judgmental" get a bad rap when it comes to relationships. The general interpretation of these words is pejorative, implying that judgment isn't just. But I would argue that judgment is an essential element of any healthy relationship. The real danger is *negative* judgment.

"Judge" is a lot like "catch." Have you ever been caught with your hand in a cookie jar? How about when you fell down the stairs? When someone catches you, it can be punitive or protective. "Pride" is another word like this. Pride can go before a fall or it can empower and encourage you. One of my favorite song lyrics comes from the song "The Perfect Space" by The Avett Brothers: *I wanna have pride like my mother has / And not like the kind in the bible that turns you bad.* You have to make sure your pride doesn't turn you bad. You have to do the same with your tendency toward judgment.

I would argue that judgment is an essential element of any healthy relationship.

I want to let you in on a little secret about therapists. Presumably, couples enter counseling to get a non-judgmental perspective about what's going on in their relationship. But the truth is, we *are* judging you. All the time. No doubt, some of my colleagues will balk at this notion, but I'm not afraid to own it. On the Myers-Briggs Type Indicator, I am an INTJ, which means that judging is who I am. In fact, I couldn't do my job without it. The capacity for judgment is a gift, even a responsibility. In the therapist's office, couples say things to me and to one another that they wouldn't consider saying at home. They feel a freedom based on the belief that in that place, their highest hopes and deepest fears can be safely expressed—and they can. But it's not because there's no judgment. It's because the judgment is measured and considered and articulated in a way that serves the relationship.

Whether you're an introvert or an extrovert, sensitive or intuitive, a thinker or a feeler, a perceiver or a judger, you can relate in a healthy way. But if your inclination is toward judgment, it helps to pay extra careful attention to a couple of the Four Horsemen. Speaking from experience, we judgers are prone to contempt and criticism. We know what's "just," so we're pretty good at pointing out what's wrong with everyone else and letting them know how to fix it. This type of judgment is dangerous because it transforms the home into a courtroom. Cases are won and lost. Verdicts are handed out. Punishments are levied. In these homes, where one partner wields judgment like a sword, both partners suffer.

The best judges get to the heart of the matter.

In law, the best judges are known for their wisdom, their patience, and their discernment. They understand and articulate the law effectively. The best judges get to the heart of the matter. Similarly, good judges in relationships understand the science of love and the art of repair. They care for the relationship more than they are preoccupied with justice. A wise judge knows that their job is to catch their loved one when falling, not simply when they've broken the law.

One of the goals of Gottman Method Couples Therapy (GMCT) is to ensure that couples do not become "therapy-dependent." To that end, the therapist equips couples with the ability to make considered decisions and come to sensible conclusions (i.e. judgments), teaching them to express those judgments in healthy, positive ways. In this way, the freedom that couples feel in the therapists' office can be replicated at home. So catch each other. Learn to judge when your partner needs space, or a hug, or a laugh. With this kind of wise, joint judgment, your home will never feel like a courtroom.

Judgment Discussion Questions:

1. Do you feel that you or your partner has a tendency toward judgment? How does it manifest?

2. What are some ways *positive* judgment has played a role in your relationships—romantic and otherwise?

3. How might negative judgment creep into a relationship unnoticed?

4. How could a tendency toward judgment actually benefit a relationship? What are the strengths of judgment?

5. Why might the "measured and considered" judgment in a therapist's allow a couple to feel free to discuss difficult issues? How can you replicate this freedom in your home?

K

K is for Kissing

My first kiss was with an older woman. At least, older in the sense that she could drive and I couldn't. It was after a football game one Friday night. We'd enjoyed a post-game meal at Arby's, loitered with friends at the firehouse, drove around, then around some more. Finally...we parked. I was terrified. All of my practicing with a Dixie cup hadn't prepared me for the real deal. Tentative, we leaned into the center of that 1990 Honda Accord and eventually, miraculously, we found each other's lips. What happened next was awkward and sloppy and gross and magical. I'll never forget it.

When was the last time you told the story of your first kiss? I bet you had a smile on your face. Kisses do that. They make us smile and swoon. They put butterflies in our stomach. They make our hairs stand up a little taller and our blood run a little faster.

And kisses are powerful! A kiss can turn a toad into a prince. It can wake a princess from eternal slumber. A kiss is art. It's poetry. It's the only appropriate response to lifting the Stanley Cup or finally returning to solid ground after a terrifying flight. A kiss inspired one of the all-time greatest lines of film dialogue from *Bull Durham*'s Crash Davis: "I believe in long, slow, deep, soft, wet kisses that last for three days." And one of the most annoyingly catchy jingles in the history of advertising: *Every Kiss Begins with Kay!* (You're welcome.) A kiss seals the deal. That's why we end weddings with a kiss, as if to say, "Okay, *now* it's official."

**Surely you remember your first kiss.
Do you remember your last kiss?**

Where does the power of a kiss come from, I wonder? Maybe hormones. Kissing releases oxytocin, which is the same hormone that is secreted when breastfeeding. Oxytocin is responsible for the comfort and connection that forms between mother and child and may explain the way kissing bonds us to another. Kissing also releases dopamine, which triggers the same part of your brain that is stimulated by cocaine. And those butterflies in your stomach? They come from epinephrine and norepinephrine, which increase your heartbeat and send oxygenated blood to your brain. Some studies have even shown that kissing can even cause a reduction in the stress hormone cortisol, so kissing could also help lower your blood pressure and prevent heart attacks.

So, kissing great because of science? Is that the secret? As it turns out, there doesn't seem to be an accepted system for how to define, collect, classify, and interpret the data of kissing. Sheril Kirshenbaum explores this in her book *The Science of Kissing* and ultimately suggests that, for the most part, scientists aren't exactly sure why we kiss.[1] Personally, I'm glad they haven't figured it out. Perhaps the power of a kiss comes, at least in part, from the mystery.

Surely you remember your first kiss. Do you remember your last kiss? Do you remember it with the same kind of nostalgia? Unlikely. For all the magic and art and poetry that's wrapped up in a kiss, I fear that in most long-term relationships, the kiss has become mundane. A perfunctory greeting at best, too often quick and passionless and tight-lipped. I know I take for granted the kisses I give and receive at the end of each day. And it's been way too long since I've simply made out with my wife. I need to change that. Do you?

Too many couples come into my office lamenting that the passion is gone from the relationship. That the fire has died. It's a common story: Life gets hectic. Work is stressful. The kitchen is a mess. The kids are...kids. I get it. But we don't have to become victims of that story. And we certainly shouldn't stop kissing. It might just be the gateway to getting that passion back.

Start simple. Even with work and kids and house and life, can you spare six seconds? John Gottman suggests that couples share a six-second kiss every day, because "a six-second kiss is a kiss with *potential*." But you don't

1. Sheril Kirshenbaum, "The Science of Kissing: What Our Lips Are Telling Us," http://www.sherilkirshenbaum.com

necessarily have to attach it to sex. In fact, don't. Let the kiss speak for itself. Let it build anticipation, distract from the day's stress, block out the whiny toddler, bring back memories of heart-racing nights. Let it remind you of past passion, even if it's hard to feel passionate sitting next to that pile of laundry. Let it feel awkward and sloppy. Let it feel too long. Or, let it go for a few more seconds. If it leads to sex, great, but don't make that the goal. Just try connecting with your partner each day with a long, slow, deep, soft, wet kiss.

The bottom line is that every marriage deserves excitement.

Try it for two weeks, and see if anything changes. Maybe it's just a shift in how you look at each other at the end of the day. Maybe you laugh more. Maybe you roll your eyes less. The bottom line is that every marriage deserves excitement, and if you feel like the passion has left yours, don't give up. The power to rekindle the fire is in your hands! Er...lips. So pucker up. It's time we reclaimed the kiss from the domain of parking teenagers and put it back into its rightful place as the official symbol of marriage.

Kissing Discussion Questions:

1. What's your first kiss story? How do you feel when you think about the story?
2. Read through the scientific effects of kissing one more time. Can you remember experiencing those effects from a kiss? When?
3. Why do you think it's important to kiss your partner passionately without sex being the goal?
4. Think about the first time you and your partner kissed, and discuss how your kissing has changed since. What has gotten better? What could benefit from revisiting that old story?
5. How often do you and your partner kiss each day? How does it feel to imagine adding a six-second "long, slow, deep, soft, wet kiss" to your routine? Can you commit to a two-week challenge?

L

L is for Love and Like

"Love" is the obvious word here. No doubt, you were expecting it. But with all due respect to love, it's probably a little *too* obvious for my tastes.

Don't get me wrong, I love love. Love has remarkable endurance. But you've heard that love covers a multitude of sins? Maybe that's the problem. The "multitude of sins" is what erodes the integrity of a relationship. I touched on this a bit in the chapter called "B is for Betrayal." As you may recall, it's not necessarily the gigantic betrayals that destroy a relationship, but the little, day-after-day ones that chip away at trust. Love, however, survives more often than it doesn't. Love is the reason couples come into my office. They are in pain precisely because they love each other—if love wasn't there, then diminished trust wouldn't be so distressing. And because love it is so foundational and so constant, it is easy to take it for granted.

The other day, my wife and I got into it. We were due for a fight and we went for it. We both raged for a hot minute. Yelled across two rooms to make sure we were "heard." She got critical. I got defensive. Typical stuff. The natural progression of a fight like this is that one of us—usually me—will at some point start cleaning the house in a huff. This time, I made the bed. Swept the kitchen. I was unloading the dishwasher when I finally ran out of steam. This, too, is typical and at this point, one of us—usually my wife—offers a hug. So we'll hug. She'll say, "I love you." I'll feel childish. We eventually reconcile. But this time when she said, "I love you," the words stung. Not because they weren't true, and not because I don't like hearing them. It's just that, I *know* my wife loves me. What I really need to know is that she *likes* me. I need to know that she enjoys, respects, admires, and appreciates me. And to be fair, I need her to know that I enjoy, respect, admire, and appreciate her.

I know my wife loves me. What I really need to know is that she likes me.

I'd be willing to bet you've heard this line before: "I still love him. I'm just not *in love* with him." It's among the most cliché of clichés—so much so that it sounds like a cop-out. What does that even mean? What's the difference between "love" and "in love"? For my part, I don't think it's necessarily a cop-out. I believe it's the difference between "love" and "like."

In "I is for Imagination," I offered a quick look at Dr. Gottman's model of the Sound Relationship House. If you take a look at the diagram in the appendix you'll notice that the bottom three levels are all about "liking" each other. More specifically, they emphasize the kind of relational friendship that is critical to building trust and intimacy:

- **Build Love Maps:** Know your partner's world. Become an expert in her likes and dislikes. Listen to his stories—several times, if necessary. Know her dreams as well as her fears. Care about and remember his favorite movies and his least favorite food.
- **Share Fondness and Admiration:** Let your partner know that you're proud of them. Notice—out loud—their creativity, intelligence, empathy. Say: "Well done," "You look hot," "Thank you."
- **Turn Towards Instead of Away:** Hold hands. Answer his questions. Ask her opinion. Laugh at his jokes. Meet her eyes.

Because they help you build a genuine friendship with your partner, these levels lead to what Gottman calls *The Positive Perspective*, or Positive Sentiment Override (PSO). In the same way that a multitude of sins chip away at a relationship, PSO protects and fortifies your friendship to help you survive those days when you're due for a fight. PSO is essential for managing and surviving conflict.

It's extremely important to say, "I love you." In fact, one of the early signs that a relationship is in trouble is that couples simply stop saying those words to each other. So please don't stop. But also, don't stop at "I love you." My wife and I survived that fight the other day, largely because we do still like each other. It was just one of those day. But those days can add up and start to feel overwhelming, so we decided to take it seriously and learned a new skill—or at least a new phrase: "I love you and I like you." Give it a try. Don't assume your partner knows. Say it a lot. It might not be as obvious, but it sure helps.

Love and Like Discussion Questions:

1. What do you see as the difference between love and like? Why are both critical in a committed relationship?
2. How can you communicate more "like" to your partner? How could your partner communicate it to you?
3. How might "building love maps" foster both love and like in your relationship? How can you add more detail to your current love maps?
4. Find something specific to praise your partner about out loud. Does it feel awkward or easy to communicate fondness and admiration to your partner? Why do you think that is? How did it make your partner feel?
5. Why do you think it's important to say the words "I love you" and "I like you" out loud to your partner? Do you say them often now? Why or why not?

M

M is for Money

At most weddings, the happy couple stands in front of their friends and family and promises to stick together, no matter what. For better and for worse. In sickness and in health. For richer and for poorer. That last one is tricky, especially considering that any time two people get hitched, one becomes richer and the other becomes poorer. It's the law of averages.

It should come as no surprise that money is one of the most common areas of marital conflict. As a therapist, the money conversation is one of my favorites to have with couples because it's the perfect playground for a discussion about solvable versus perpetual problems. You see, money is never just money.

First, and most simply, money is math. $1 + $1 = $2. You can use that $2 to buy a thing that costs $2. If you spend less than $2, you have money left over. If you spend more than $2, you owe somebody money. And while I personally do not know how to calculate simple interest, I do know that earning and paying interest on money you save and owe is subject to fundamental mathematical rules. In the mathematical sense, money is actually pretty easy.

But money isn't just math, is it? It's loaded. It has meaning. You and your partner likely have different ideas about what a dollar is worth and where it should go. You have different ideas about savings, and debt, and wealth, and poverty. What does $2 represent? Is it security? Luxury? Power? Until you understand the meaning you place on your money—no matter how much or how little you may have—the actual math isn't very helpful.

Until you understand the meaning you place on your money—no matter how much or how little you may have—the actual math isn't very helpful.

To clarify this point, imagine your income were to increase right now by 20 percent. First, do you know how much of a raise you'd be getting? That's the *math*. Second, what would you do with the extra money? That's the *meaning*.

It's important to have these conversations early, because sorting out the math only exposes the need to create shared meaning around money. In my practice, I've found that I have the money conversation most often with pre-married couples and newlyweds. There's a special place in my heart for these couples. On my imaginary list of "Top 5 Regrets from My First Year of Marriage" I would have to include not meeting with, and listening to, a financial advisor.

There's a litany of reasons we didn't make this a priority, but it boiled down to feeling hopeless about the math. I was unemployed, swimming in debt, and uncertain about my financial hopes and dreams. But our fear of the conversation cost us. If you haven't done it already, I encourage you talk with someone who can help you understand the math and meaning of money, especially if you're just getting started. The healthiest couples are in agreement about where they hold value in their household. This agreement is essential when navigating the many economies at play in the relationship.

Yes, economies. How do you as a couple, family, and household deal with your limited resources? There is, of course, the economy of the dollar bill. But there are also economies of attention, affection, time, energy, and labor, among others. The cost of paying someone to do yard work may offset the emotional and/or physical cost of spending a day in the dirt. You may have to weigh the value of a once-in-a-lifetime family vacation against the fact that you'd need to put the bulk of it on a credit card. Understanding the economies that exist for you and your family will help you make those tough choices.

In any case, the money that moves in and out of your household budget should serve to support and enhance your core values as a couple. You just need to know what those values are. You might agree that savings are important, but you may not agree on what you're saving for. A car? A house? College for your children? European vacation? You may need to have the same conversation about whether you will prioritize philanthropy. Will you give a portion of your income to charity? How much? To which charities? Why? Personally, I'm a champion of philanthropic intent in your financial planning, in part because it's the one thing that has changed the way my wife and I think about money. In choosing to give away our money, we've discovered that not only does it have less power over us, but we're also more able to clarify the meaning of the money we do have.

Understanding the economies that exist for you and your family will help you make those tough choices.

In the end, as important as it is to get your finances in order, it's just as important to remember that richer and poorer may have very little to do with math. According to Dr. Gottman in *The Seven Principles for Making Marriage Work*, "What's most important in terms of your marriage is that you work as a team on financial issues and that you express your concerns, needs, and fantasies to each other before coming up with a plan." In other words, working together to craft your financial future and create shared meaning within those finances is, by far, the smartest investment you'll ever make.

Money Discussion Questions:

1. Why is it important to consider both math and meaning when planning your finances together?
2. Consider the exercise suggested in this section. What would you do with a 20 percent increase in income? How would you adjust if your income decreased by 20 percent? What do your answers say about the meaning you place on your finances?
3. Think about some recent financial decisions. What *economies* informed your choices?
4. Have you and your partner discussed the meaning and value of your finances? If so, what have you learned about each other from these conversations? If not, what do you think holds you back?
5. Make a list if your concerns, needs, and fantasies surrounding your financial future. Compare your list with your partner's, and discuss where they are similar and different. How will your combined lists inform your financial planning as a couple?

N

N is for Newlyweds

Newlyweds. The word inspires song-written images of carefree Sundays that begin with playful games of "Guess Who Cooks?" and end with reading poetry from overdue library books under the apple tree in the backyard (credit to singer/songwriter David Harris for that one). Our first year wasn't like that. We did have an apple tree in the backyard of our first rental house, but we also had a moldy basement.

I do a fair bit of pre-marital counseling in my practice and lately my philosophy is shifting. I used to work through a pre-established set of topics to help couples prepare for marriage. At the end of six sessions, we'd check the box and the happy couple would skip off to marital bliss. The problem with this sort of pre-marital counseling is that it implies that you can prepare for marriage before you're actually married. But I don't think that's possible or healthy.

More recently, I've been asking couples to throw out the notion of pre-marital therapy and think instead of "transition to marriage" therapy. Giving couples an extended vision for therapy helps cement the preparation and acknowledges that the only thing that can prepare you for marriage is actually being married. There may be "Seven Principles for Making Marriage Work", but in my work with newlyweds I focus on priorities more than principles. So, without further ado, here are:

Four Priorities for Newlyweds

1. Have a Thing: In the Gottman vernacular this would be "Create Shared Meaning." Basically, it's the idea that couples need to get proactive about forming a marriage culture that is uniquely their own. We spend most of our lives forming our identities through our family of origin. Then, one day we decide to get married and have to take on a new identity. I encourage couples to start by Having a Thing. Sometimes it's the creation of a ritual—like Saturday morning hikes. Sometimes it's the cultivation of a value—like generosity or hospitality. Sometimes it's agreeing on a dream and working toward it—like a 5 year anniversary trip to Ireland. In order to have a thing *together* you have to get to know your partner's hopes and fears, you have to focus your vision, and you may have to make sacrifices. But overall, Having a Thing is a fun and relatively easy thing to prioritize.

2. Fight Fair: Again, in the Gottman vernacular, this would be "Managing Conflict." There's a reason that songwriters are drawn to carefree Sundays rather than stress-filled Mondays. Conflict isn't poetic, but that doesn't mean it can't be artfully done. It is important for couples to recognize that conflict is inevitable and that the sooner they identify their problem issues, the better. The hardest lesson I learned during my first year of marriage was how selfish I was. I wasn't very good at picking my battles and so we fought about everything from how to spend money to where to store the toothbrushes. When couples do the hard work of understanding the anatomy of their conflict and establishing healthy patterns of relating, it can help secure the foundation of the relationship in the long run. Fighting fair is a less fun, but arguably more intimate, priority for the first year.

Fighting fair is a less fun, but arguably more intimate, priority for the first year.

3. Collect Resources: In "M is for Money," I mentioned that you need to find a financial advisor. Money is just one example of what I mean by resources. Perhaps it goes without saying, but I think you should also find a good therapist—one for each of you and one for your relationship. Get to know your neighbors. Get a library card. Take a cooking class. Basically, get to know your community and the resources that are available therein. Marriages aren't meant to exist in a vacuum, and knowing where and how to get help from (and give help to) your community can go long way—especially when the newlywed phase fades into the "we've been married a while, now what?" phase.

4. No Regret: All things considered, this may not belong on the list. Some of the most successful pre-marital therapy concludes with the couple deciding not to marry. Or at least not yet. Marriage is hard work and you're bound to make mistakes. Regrets are okay. *Regret* is another thing altogether. I hear way too many stories of divorcing couples who say things like "I ignored the warning signs" or, "We shouldn't have gotten married in the first place." Don't ignore the warning signs. Keep your eyes open for the Four Horsemen of the Apocalypse and rein them in.

When the shine of that first year starts to fade, when Monday arrives asking for those overdue library book fines, when mold shows up in the basement, what can you fall back on? Even if you've been married or partnered for a while, take time to make sure those first three priorities are sound so the fourth doesn't seep in at the first sign of challenges. Early in Gottman Method Couples Therapy, we ask this question: *If you had your life to live over again, do you think you would: (a) marry the same person (b) marry a different person (c) not marry at all?* Be sure to give your relationship the scrutiny it deserves so that five, fifteen, fifty years later you can answer (a) with confidence and conviction.

Newlyweds Discussion Questions:

1. If you are married or in a long-term partnership, how did you prepare for that kind of commitment? If you're not married, how do you think you would prepare?
2. Do you and your partner "have a thing"? What is it, and how do you think it benefits your relationship?
3. How do you and your partner manage conflict? What works? How do you think you could improve?
4. Aside from finances, what would it look like for you and your partner to "collect resources"? What resources have you already gathered? What might you need more of?
5. Think about regrets you may have in your relationship. Discuss with your partner how you can keep these regrets from turning into *regret* down the road.

O

O is for Opportunity

Whenever I work with pre-marital couples, we spend a fair bit of time pondering what a marriage actually is. Is it a social contract? A political statement? A business agreement? A holy sacrament? All of the above? We explore whether marriage is a right, a privilege, a gift, a responsibility, a burden—there's a reason the ball-and-chain metaphor exists. Mostly, we work on exposing the attitudes, biases, and expectations for the relationship. And while everyone should at the very least understand that marriage is complicated, I would say that marriage is, above all, an *opportunity*.

Dr. Gottman's Four Horsemen of the Apocalypse alludes to a prophecy in the book of Revelation—the last book of the Bible. But there's some ancient wisdom from the first book of the Bible as well. In the book of Genesis, Adam and Eve go through a bit of pre-marital counseling, wherein God explains the opportunities inherent in marriage. He defines marriage to be when "a man leaves his father and mother and is united to his wife, and they become one flesh." (Genesis 2:24 NIV)

Leaving theology and gender issues aside for the moment, let's take a look at the wisdom in this definition:

1. Leave Home: One of the reasons that Dr. Gottman's Sound Relationship House metaphor is so effective is that it implies a structure that belongs to you and your spouse alone. Every structure needs sturdy walls, and the only way to build a Sound Relationship House together is to ensure that you've constructed healthy boundaries around your relationship. This starts with Mom and Dad.

Now, I'm not advising that you shut yourselves off from your parents as soon as the vows are over. But marriage is an opportunity to declare that someone else is taking the role of "the man in your life" (or the woman, of course), and to arrange your life, attention, and priorities accordingly. It's tough to "leave" your mother and father, especially if they are good, attentive parents who have loved and supported you throughout your life. I've actually found it can be more difficult to leave parents who were less than perfect or even harmful. But either way, it's critical to creating a strong, new family that's built upon the values you and your spouse cherish.

Leaving home isn't just about your parents. It also includes your old boyfriends and girlfriends. Maybe the band you were in during college. Maybe the fact that you usually spend every Saturday with your sister. It could be the actual physical structures that you are living in. Shirley Glass has famously noted that the healthiest relationships happen when partners keep a window open between each other while erecting walls that protect their privacy from the outside world.[1] Relationships get in trouble when walls and windows reverse and boundaries become unclear. Think of your marriage as an *opportunity* to draw healthy boundaries and build a strong foundation for your very own home.

2. Seek Unity: Most of us want to find a compatible partner, someone who also likes chocolate and Ghostbusters and long walks on the beach. But I think compatibility is overrated. What's required is unity. Unity doesn't mean you're the *same*; it means you're *together*. The top level of the Sound Relationship House focuses on creating shared meaning. Don't underestimate the value of this opportunity.

Unity doesn't mean you're the *same*; it means you're *together*.

With the confidence that comes from healthy boundaries, you can take creative risks in establishing new rituals that will bond you together. How will you make the holidays uniquely your own? Get ambitious about setting goals. Where will celebrate your fifth, tenth, and fiftieth anniversaries? You can be courageous about defining (and re-defining) your roles in the relationship. Who cleans this week? What happens when we switch the bread-winner role?

1. Shirley Glass, Not Just Friends (New York: Free Press, 2003).

Unity means defining together the ideas of home and money and family and sex and autonomy, and even unity itself. This is hard work, because it means giving up some of your own ideas in order to accept your spouse's. If I've said it once, I've said it a whole bunch: the hardest lesson I learned during my first year of marriage was how selfish I was. Unity means letting go of your selfishness in order to become a better version of yourself. Again, what a wonderful *opportunity*.

3. Have Sex: This may seem like a no-brainer, and indeed, you may already be having sex, but "becoming one flesh" is a specific invitation to have *married* sex. I'm not trying to spark a moral debate, but I do think there is something inherently different—and inherently better—about married sex. Even Hollywood may have figured this out. Think of all the times you've ever seen two people making love on screen, either explicit or implied. Now, how many of those scenes depicted married people having sex *with each other*? Pretty small percentage, I bet. Hollywood is either implying that married sex isn't sexy, or that it's somehow too sacred to use for selling commercial time.

The Gottmans have done a beautiful job advocating for married sex that is both sexy and sacred. They argue for "personal sex" by shifting the focus away from intercourse and toward intimacy. Dr. Gottman is a champion for erotic and emotionally connected sex that comes from a strong sense of trust and commitment. Indeed, you should practice the techniques of sex. But think of your marriage as an *opportunity* to have different—and better—sex by focusing on your long-term friendship and emotional connection.

Regardless of how you feel about the Bible, it offers some important wisdom about how we are meant to be in relationship with one another. Genesis gives us a glimpse of what a marriage should be. Revelation reminds us of what it shouldn't.

I do think there is something inherently different—and inherently better—about married sex.

But let's take the Bible out of it and weigh the opportunities available to anyone willing to commit to a long-term relationship. There's a freedom that comes from leaving home and establishing healthy boundaries. There's an exhilaration and maturation that comes from seeking unity by creating shared meaning and establishing new patterns. There's an intimacy that comes from investing in emotional connection and prioritizing personal sex. If every opportunity comes with a cost, then in this case it's the work of exposing your attitudes, biases, and expectations for your relationship and letting go of selfishness. In return you get the materials to build your very own Sound Relationship House. As costs go, it's a pretty great value.

Opportunity Discussion Questions:

1. What does it look like for you, personally, to "leave home" when building a life with your partner? Why is that important to your relationship?

2. What are some things you and your partner have done to create shared meaning? How have these things built unity in your relationship?

3. If "personal sex" changes the focus from intercourse to intimacy, how might that lead to better (i.e. sexy *and* sacred) sex overall?

4. What do you say marriage is? If you have been married or partnered for a long time, do you think your definition would have been different early on? If you are newlyweds, go through the first paragraph and discuss how each definition resonates with you.

5. Think about the costs vs. opportunities in a marriage or committed relationship. What have you, personally, had to give up? What did you get in return? What might you still need to expose or relinquish?

P

P is for Problems

As you may remember from "A is for Arguments," John Gottman's research has revealed that about two-thirds of relationship problems are unsolvable. He calls these perpetual problems—the ones you'll probably still be fussing about five years from now even though you were fussing about them five years ago. One of my favorite questions for couples is whether that statistic is *discouraging* or *encouraging*. Think about that for a second. Does it bum you out that 69 percent of your issues are not going away? Or does it give you hope?

If you can accept that many of your problems aren't going away, then you can focus on what to do about those issues when they come up.

Most couples I know are frustrated to think that most of their problems are unsolvable. It's hard to have the same battles over and over again. My personal bias, however, is that I'm glad to know that we're normal. In my own marriage, for example, a recurring irritant is the fact that one of us is an extrovert—life of the party, lights up a room, and all that—and the other is an off-the-charts introvert. We still haven't figured out how to make each other go to a party the right way, but it's nice to know that we're not alone in our fruitless efforts.

According to Dr. Gottman, the number one thing that couples fight about is *nothing*. I can vouch for this, too! This past weekend, my wife and I got into a heated argument over fruit flies. Seriously. Later, when our older daughter (age 11) was explaining the argument to her sister (age 7), she said, "It's never about the fruit flies." If she's right (and she is) then what's it really about?

I think it's about *perspective* (bonus P-word). If you can accept that many of your problems aren't going away, then you can focus on what to do about those issues when they come up. As a first step, quit trying to solve the problem. It's wasted energy. Instead, focus on achieving perspective, empathy, and dialogue. It may help to think of the problem as a physical *thing* in the room, trying to distract and disgust you—kind of like fruit flies. That thing is designed to disrupt the comfort of the home with the accumulation of small annoyances that become an infestation. In the case of fruit flies, there are a bunch of home remedies (we use a glass of red wine covered with Saran wrap), but it's always better to attack the breeding ground (usually a sink drain, just FYI.) In your relationship, you can attack small annoyances every time they come up, but in order for those annoyances to fade completely, it's critical to address the deeper problem. To do that, you have to work together.

That's what dialogue is. It's a conversation *with* one another—rather than at one another—that is designed to reveal the deeper meaning of a particular conflict. Dr. Gottman refers to this as the "dream within conflict." Whenever one or both partners' dream or hope or aspiration for the relationship is ignored, problems arise. But when those dreams are revealed and understood and respected, it creates space for the relationship to become more meaningful than the problem.

Whenever one or both partners' dream or hope or aspiration for the relationship is ignored, problems arise.

Dr. Gottman suggests becoming a "Dream Detective." Try this exercise: think through some of your perpetual problems. See if you can recognize patterns within the conflicts that you've been rehashing without progress. Next, make up a brief, new story that may explain your own dream or position within that particular conflict. What hidden meaning are you trying to express? Is it connected to something in your childhood? Is it rooted in anxiety or fear? Does it stem from a previous relationship expectation? Once you've crafted your own narrative, try doing the same for your partner. Get curious about their dream or position. See if you can articulate what deeper meaning may exist for them. Try comparing notes after you've both done the exercise and see if it doesn't create new dialogue around an ancient issue. This process, called Overcoming Gridlock, is one of Gottman's *Seven Principles for Making Marriage Work.*

It bears noting that we've only addressed perpetual problems, which means we're still left with another one-third of all problems. These qualify as "solvable problems" and Dr. Gottman recommends, simply, that you solve them. There is, of course, a science and an art to this, and sometimes therapy should play a role, but identifying which problems you can solve and which require more patience is a great first step.

I'll let you guess which one of us is the life of the party and which one is the party-pooper. Suffice to say, we gave up trying to convert one another many years ago. Now we can go out with friends and each settle into our respective roles. We've learned to accept and appreciate that we each get something different out of the same environment and that's okay. By choosing to appreciate our differences—and our dreams—we've been able to eliminate pointless fussing and more fully enjoy one another.

Problems Discussion Questions:

1. Do you think that about two-thirds of your conflicts are perpetual? Why do you think that?
2. Think about some "small annoyances" that have led to conflict in your relationship. What might be the underlying problem or problems?
3. Are the problems from question two solvable or perpetual? How can you tell the difference?
4. Complete the "Dream Detective" exercise. What surprised you about your and/or your partner's dreams for the relationship? How have these dreams been appreciated or ignored? What's been the result?
5. Think about a perpetual problem in your relationship. What might it look like to *appreciate* the differences at the root of the problem, without trying to change each other?

Q

Q is for Questions

This book started as a blog series. At one point, I opened my column to questions from the public, excited to build a sense of community with my readers. I have to confess, I was really hoping to get a bunch of benign inquiries like: *What's your favorite novel? Where did you honeymoon? Cats or dogs?*

But the questions were not benign. They were filled with pain and longing and betrayal and confusion. I grieved for my readers, sorry that their relationships were struggling. I felt sad that they were not enjoying the fruits of intimate, trusting, joyful relationships.

NOTE: *All names and identifying information have been changed. Some questions have been edited for brevity.*

Peter lamented, "*Affection, touch, sex. I want it. She does not...almost never. 1-2x a year at best. No kissing, no touching, I've pretty much given up after years of rejection.*" *Then he asked, simply,* "*Why?*"

An almost identical question came from Annie, "*My spouse has put me in the Friend Zone—wants to be friends, co-parent, cohabitate, hang out—but without romance, passion, or even lovemaking. We're only 40!" She asks, "What can we do to 'fall in love' again?"*

Why? What can we do? Simple questions, but devastating and important questions.

The honest truth is that there aren't simple answers to these questions. Part of what makes satisfying relationships so rewarding is that they're hard to create and maintain. When you lose focus on the relationship, even for a moment, you can slide into habitual patterns of disconnecting pretty easily without noticing. No couple ever woke up one day and decided to stop being affectionate. They accepted, sometime much earlier in the relationship, that intimacy wasn't a priority. This is incredibly subtle and can be seen in Dr. Gottman's theory of bids and turning toward. (For more detail, check out T is for Turning.)

Part of what makes satisfying relationships so rewarding is that they're hard to create and maintain.

Both Peter and Annie are describing relationships where at least one partner has stopped making bids, likely because the other partner stopped turning toward previous bids. *Why?* Who knows? That's part of why therapy is really helpful. *What can we do?* Start by focusing on bids. First focus on turning toward your partner's bids. Let them know that you're paying attention to them. That you think they're interesting, funny, attractive. Then re-evaluate your own strategy for bids for affection and attention. Get really good at holding hands, then hugging, then the six-second kiss. It's important to have patience with yourself and with your partner during this process. The relationship got knocked off-track way back when, and it'll take hard work to get back to where you deserve. But you can get there. It's the tortoise's work, not the hare's.

If there was one dominant topic in the questions I received, it was jealousy and betrayal. Specifically, how to avoid jealousy and recover from betrayal. These issues, just like the intimacy questions above, ultimately boil down to how well a couple can make and respond to bids for affection and attention. When you do that well, you will protect yourself from the perils of infidelity. When you don't, you sow the seeds for small betrayals that can eventually lead to infidelity. But what about after the affair?

Sarah wrote that she and her husband have been recovering well in the aftermath of his affair. They've both done a great job taking responsibility and re-investing in their friendship. They are talking together and working through conflict more often and better than before. Still, they're having a hard time trusting in the "new norm." "*How long*," she asks, "*does it take to create lasting overall confidence and trust?*"

Of course it would be silly to try and offer a precise timeline, but I tend to think it boils down to perspective. The further away you get from the incident, the more it fades into distant memory. It's natural to have some post-traumatic stress in the wake of an affair and to continue to struggle with confidence and security, but at some point, the perspective (and the story) will shift away from the betrayal and toward the recovery. The Gottmans refer to a process of Atonement, Attunement, Attachment. Trust that process and continue to lean into the new norm. At some level, simply committing makes it so.

Secure attachment goes a long way toward mitigating jealousy even when infidelity has never been an issue. Justin asks, "*How do I lovingly connect to my jealous wife while not giving up who I am and what I enjoy?*" I suppose it really depends on who you are and what you enjoy, as certainly some things are inappropriate. But the best way to lovingly connect with your wife is to discover your wife's dream and honor it. Her jealousy is attached to some portion of her dream that has not been heard or respected. If you want to mitigate betrayal in your relationship, focus on appreciating that dream.

The final theme that came up in your questions, and perhaps the most telling, is how important it is for you to be heard. More than a few of you sent me paragraphs about your relationship. I imagine it must have felt good to know that someone, anyone, was willing to hear your story and offer empathy and insight. Or maybe just the act of writing down your story helped you make sense of it. In any case, I want to encourage you to consider therapy as a means to understand your struggle. A good therapist is infinitely more effective than some guy sitting at a keyboard.

Cheryl wrote, "*My husband is so controlling, at this present moment he hasn't been talking to me for two weeks now. He even moved out of our bedroom and stopped eating my food. The only time he talks to me or things are normal is when I compromise my happiness and do what he wants, and I am tired of living my live through making him happy at the expense of my happiness."*

Ashley said, "*My husband and I have been married for 15 years and been experts in the four horseman since we walked down the aisle. We've lived parallel lives for most of our marriage. Lately, we've been trying to stop the four horseman cycle, to nurture our fondness and admiration and turn toward each other. It's not working well enough (yet) for me to imagine staying in this marriage much longer.*"

Cheryl and Ashley are asking the same questions: *Can my marriage be saved? When is enough enough? Are my expectations too high? Help.*

I can tell you this for sure: you are not alone.

The hard truth is that sometimes, the answer is "No, your marriage cannot be saved. 'Enough' was a long time ago. Yes, your expectations are too high." Most couples are unhappy for an average of six years before they seek help. Even then it could be too late. Dr. Gottman often refers to the "Story of Us." If your "Story of Us" is fraught with contempt rather than admiration, more "me" than "we," and more disappointment than satisfaction, it may be time to try telling a different story.

Dr. Gottman says, "If there is clear compelling evidence that your relationship is already over or unsalvageable, and you want to move on, I believe it's okay to let it go." I agree. Even as a relationship therapist, I'm not in the "Stay Married At All Costs" camp. But I'd urge you to get some help before you decide to walk away. A good therapist will help you identify the strengths in the relationship that may simply be hiding in the midst of present chaos. It can be helpful to have an outside eye discern the baby from the bathwater. Minimally, it'll be a good opportunity to tell your "Story of Us" and get some insight and empathy. Check the Gottman Referral Network (gottmanreferralnetwork.com) to see if there's a good Gottman-trained therapist in your area.

I can tell you this for sure: you are not alone. I get questions like yours all the time. I hear stories of pain and longing and betrayal and confusion. But I also see couples recover and reclaim the best of themselves and their relationship. Again, it's the tortoise's work, not the hare's.

By the way, my favorite novel is *The Brothers K* by David James Duncan, my wife and I honeymooned in Bermuda, and I don't have the pet gene, so my preference with regard to cats and dogs is "neither." If you have any other questions, big or small, my contact information is at the end of this book. I can't guarantee any easy answers. But I would love to hear from you.

Questions Discussion Questions:

1. When questions and concerns arise in your relationship, whom do you typically talk to? Why do you choose them? Do you feel that these conversations are beneficial or harmful to your relationship?

2. What questions are you currently asking about your relationship? Have you discussed these questions with your partner? How might the topics addressed in this chapter be helpful?

3. What do you think Gottman means when he says "Atonement, Attunement, Attachment" can lead to a new norm? What would that look like for you?

4. Think about your "Story of Us." What parts make you smile? What questions surface?

5. Have you and your partner ever attended therapy—either together or separately? If so, how did you respond to it? If not, is it something you would consider? Why or why not?

R

R is for Repair

Repair is easily my favorite concept in the entire Gottman encyclopedia. Typically, we think of repair in terms of what we have to do to a car or a washing machine or a botched haircut. Something has broken, so we need to repair it. But in relational terms, repair is less about fixing what's broken and more about getting back on track.

Finding the repair strategies that work for you can actually be a unique game that belongs to just the two of you.

Masters of relationships repair early and often, and they have lots of strategies for how to do it. Dr. Gottman describes a repair attempt as "any statement or action, silly or otherwise, that prevents negativity from escalating out of control." The reason I love the concept so much is because of the word "any." It leaves a ton of room for creativity. Because every relationship is different, finding the repair strategies that work for you can actually be a unique game that belongs to just the two of you.

Of course, you have to be in the right frame of mind to play. Whenever our family has an especially long, stressful, tiring day—the kind of day where nothing goes right and we're all about to tear each others' heads off—my seven-year-old will, without fail, ask to "play a family game." It's her own attempt at repair I guess, but man those games are tough. Sometimes it's hard to rally for Go Fish.

So how do you get into mindset for a repair attempt? There's a book I love that was given to me by one of my favorite therapists. (As in, one of my favorite therapists who was actually my therapist.) The book is called *Finite and Infinite Games* by James Carse. In his central thesis, Carse argues that human beings are constantly playing one of two kinds of games: you guessed it—finite and infinite. You can and should buy and read this book as soon as possible, but in the meantime I'll outline his basic points.

In a finite game the boundaries are very clear. Rules are predetermined, and when a player violates the rule he is penalized. The game has a specific time limit and the object of the game is to win. It's football. American Ninja Warrior. The stock market. But in an infinite game, there is no time limit and the boundaries are fluid. The rules are made up by the players and can change at any time, so that the goal is not to win, but to prolong the game. It's the game of life, or for our purposes, the game of relationships. Carse also suggests that, "whoever *must* play, cannot *play*."[1] This notion speaks to the value of cooperation, intentionality, and agreement. Players (partners) can't be forced to conform to an unknown or unstated set of rules, but instead must work together to draft rules that ensure the continuation of the game (the relationship).

Repair is ultimately about rules. More specifically, it's about making rules together. The Gottman library of interventions includes a "Repair Checklist"—a list of phrases clustered into different categories, such as I FEEL, SORRY, and GET TO YES. The idea is that as conversations escalate, you can turn to the list and identify which phrases will and won't work. I especially like the category called STOP ACTION, which is designed to interrupt the escalation of an argument before one or both partners gets flooded and redirects the conversation. There are a dozen or so phrases to choose from and the "game" is looking at the list together and deciding what might or might not work. You might decide together, "I really like #3, #6 and #11; I think those will help me calm down. But I do not like #10. If you use that phrase with me it'll only make it worse." (It should be noted that "calm down" is not on the list of suggestions because "calm down" never works for anyone ever. Don't use it.) This process of engaging the Repair Checklist is a great example of shaping and prolonging an infinite game by making rules together.

---

1. James P. Carse, Finite and Infinite Games (New York: Random House, 1987), (Henry James, The Ambassadors (Rockville: Serenity, 2009), 34-40.

But you're not limited to the checklist. I have a couple in my practice that met at a Super Bowl party, and one of their stop action techniques is to "throw a flag." Actually, those quotation marks are misleading. They literally have a yellow flag like football officials use and either partner can throw the flag at any time to keep an argument from escalating. And it works! It works because they agreed together to create and follow that rule.

Statistically, a marriage can survive The Four Horsemen of the Apocalypse, but only if partners learn to repair effectively.

No matter what strategies you choose, it is absolutely critical that you master the art of making and receiving repair attempts. In Gottman's research, the consistent failure of repair attempts is a sign of an unhappy future. Statistically, a marriage can survive The Four Horsemen of the Apocalypse, but only if partners learn to repair effectively. Without that, you risk settling into a finite game where, even when one partner "wins," you both end up losing.

Don't get me wrong—I'm not pretending that building a foundation for repair is easy. Playing the infinite game is complicated because creativity is always complicated. But start small. Remember Gottman's caveat that *any* action or statement includes those "silly or otherwise." So have fun brainstorming what will work for you. Create rules that have significant meaning to the two of you, and don't worry if it feels like nonsense. If it makes you laugh, all the better! Does it seem ironic that play is the real work of the relationship? Maybe. But if you truly invest in the game, embracing the rules and signposts you build together along the way, you reap the very serious mutual benefit of prolonging your relationship through increased trust and intimacy. And that's well worth a couple rounds of Go Fish.

Repair Discussion Questions:

1. Why is it important to view the concept of Repair as "getting back on track" rather than "fixing something that's broken?"
2. Can you identify some repair attempts that you have tried, with your partner and/or in other important relationships (work, family, friends, etc.)? Were they successful? Why or why not?
3. What are some rules that already exist in the infinite game of your relationship?
4. Are there any rules in your relationship that you feel need some improvement? How might they work better?
5. Write your own list of "STOP ACTION" phrases or actions with your partner. Think about what typically refocuses you when you feel heated. Humor? Reassurance? Physical touch? Be creative!

S

S is for Sex

The idea of me writing about sex is kind of comical. My wife will be the first to tell you that I don't possess any particular expertise. It's not a criticism. It's just part of the simple truth that despite almost two decades of practice, we haven't yet mastered what Drs. John and Julie Gottman have dubbed *The Art and Science of Lovemaking*.

Good sex is very much interrelated with intimate trust, friendship, and conversations that create emotional connection.

In their *Gott Sex?* series, the Gottmans have suggested that the best sex tends to be a result of the strongest friendships. As they prepared to write *And Baby Makes Three*, Dr. John Gottman and his research team interviewed couples about sex and intimacy shortly after they had their first baby. I was fortunate enough to be part of that team, which ultimately confirmed the hypothesis that good sex is very much interrelated with intimate trust, friendship, and conversations that create emotional connection.

This may not seem like earth-shattering information, but it also doesn't quite line up with the thousands of contrary messages we receive about sex each day. I don't know about you, but my sex life doesn't look anything like the stuff I see on HBO or even in the commercials during the Seahawks game. I call that "sexy sex" and it's too simple. Most of the actual sex I'm familiar with is complicated. It's risky. But ultimately, it's more rewarding than anything on TV.

So, with apologies to any of you looking for advice about how to have more "sexy sex," here are some thoughts on actual, real-life lovemaking.

Talking about sex is more intimate than having sex

Turns out, the most important part of cultivating a healthy sex life is talking about a healthy sex life. Only 9 percent of couples who can't comfortably talk about sex with one another say that they're satisfied sexually. OK, easy solution, right? Just talk! But have you ever tried talking about your sexual preferences, your fears, your hopes? Have you ever told your partner your sexual story? Not the story of your triumphs—the story of how you learned about sex, how you became aware of your sexuality, how you experienced the pain and shame, but also the joy and beauty, of sex.

It's tough. It's not typical dinner table conversation,

especially if your kids are around. And it's not something you can check off the list while running errands. I don't recommend texting or instant messaging about these most intimate details. And probably the worst time to attempt this kind of conversation is *during* sex. Talking about sex deserves an intimate, dedicated time and space, and it should be a priority.

To get started, the Gottmans recommend creating Love Maps of your and your partner's sexuality. A "Love Map" is Gottman lingo for the practice of developing an ever clearer appreciation of your partner by continually seeking deeper understanding of their inner world. If you're new to this concept, start simple. To create a Love Map of your partner's sexuality, you don't have to go straight to questions of technique. Try this one:

There is an old saying that some partners want sex to feel close, but others only want sex when they already feel close. Does that fit us in any way? Do you think that's true? Is it true of us? Is that a problem? If so, how can we make that better?

Do the work of cultivating intimacy in order to increase the quality of your intercourse. That said...

Intimacy is more important than intercourse

We've been conditioned to think about sex in terms of quantity and quality of *intercourse.* At the micro level, we're primed to think about quantity and quality of *orgasm.* This emphasis misses the mark in both cases. Sex isn't about the act. Or rather, sex isn't only about the act. It is also and primarily about the connection.

There are seasons of life when capacity and tolerance for sex fluctuates. The mark of a healthy sex life cannot be measured by a number. If it were, then post-partum moms and men with erectile dysfunction would be in big trouble, not to mention the depressed, the distracted, the deployed, etc. Even when sex (or orgasm) is impossible, intimacy is critical. This is where talking about sex comes in handy—but not just talking. Hugging, holding hands, snuggling, and kissing all foster intimacy. So does conflict and resolution. So does growing old together. A commitment to intimacy can yield more frequent and more satisfying sex, but even when it doesn't, intimacy remains and ultimately trumps intercourse.

Impersonal sex is more fun than personal sex

Yep, you read that right. Impersonal sex is indeed more fun, in the way that a roller coaster is more fun than a hot-air balloon ride around the globe. (The latter may not seem like fun to you, but you get my meaning.) Impersonal sex, or what Dr. Gottman calls, "erotic activity not founded on emotional connection and adoration of the partner" is always more fun. After all, it doesn't involve the hard work of intimacy building.

At this point, it's probably clear that I don't think fun is the point. The point—in committed relationships—is sharing the body, the mind, and dare I say, the soul. That's not "fun." It's difficult and risky. Learning how to initiate (and refuse) sex is work. Getting to know your partner's dreams, preferences, and body is work. Overcoming resistance, fear, and shame is work. Improving your technique is work. But while personal sex is definitely work, it's so much better. It's rich and meaningful and romantic and memorable. Couples who are committed to improving their intimate, passionate, and sexual lives with one another don't have to settle for simply fun sex.

While personal sex is definitely work, it's so much better.

So, back to the idea of me writing about sex. Believe it or not, it was pretty risky for me. I really wanted to write about Stonewalling. But I know that my ongoing sexual journey requires me to continue to do the work of leaning into intimacy and making personal sex a priority. Sometime soon, my wife will read this manuscript and shortly thereafter, I suspect we'll be having a talk. That's risky. But I'm ready. And I'm looking forward to reaping the benefits of our hard work together.

Sex Discussion Questions:

1. How do you and your partner talk about sex? What do you discuss when you do?

2. How is your sex life satisfying? In what ways could it improve? How easy is it to address these topics with your partner?

3. Why is intimacy different from intercourse? How do you and your partner foster intimacy outside of intercourse in your relationship?

4. Do you agree that "impersonal sex is more fun than personal sex"? Do you agree that personal sex is work? Why or why not?

5. When you think about your own sexual story, what do you wish your partner knew? What would be difficult to tell them? How might sharing these stories enrich your sex life?

T

T is for Turning

I have this picture in my brain. It's kind-of a flowchart for handling problems. Maybe it's a Venn diagram. At any rate, I'm going to try and explain it in writing. See if your brain can picture it too.

First, imagine the word **Problems** in the center of the page. We've already established that all relationships are going to have **Problems**. We've also explored the concept of **Repair**, which is the key to addressing the **Conflict** that arises from your Problems. A couple can respond to Problems with Conflict or with **Dialogue**. Dialogue is good. It helps you avoid **Gridlock**. Conflict is not good, but it's also not deadly. A couple can respond to Conflict with **Escalation** or Repair.

Now imagine the second part of that paragraph (from Repair on) is to the right of Problems. In "R is for Repair," we got a notion of how Repair helps return the relationship to stability—and we established that it's is my favorite concept in the Gottman lexicon. My second favorite concept is **Turning**. If Repair is the tool for diffusing Conflict, Turning is the tool for avoiding it.

Turning is on the left side of the picture.

To understand Turning, you have to first understand **Bids**. I've brought this up before, but to explain further, a Bid is any gesture—verbal or nonverbal—intended to make a positive connection with your partner. Bids can be simple or complex and can represent a request for conversation, humor, affection, support, or simply attention. Most are actually pretty easy to spot and respond to: *"How do I look?" "Can you pass the guacamole?" "Will you help me change the bedspread?"* Other bids are more complicated: *"Want to go to yoga with me?" "Let's learn how to play the guitar." "Do you feel like fooling around?"*

No matter the nature of the Bid, it is critical to learn to recognize and **Turn Toward** your partner. Dr. Gottman's research revealed that masters of relationships turn toward their spouses approximately twenty times more than couples in distress. In a newlywed study, couples who were still married six years after their wedding had turned toward each other 86 percent of the time, while those who were divorced within six years turned toward each other just 33 percent of the time.

Turning Toward is clearly best, but it can't be assumed. The concept of Turning is fraught with its own complexities. In addition to Turning Toward, partners can **Turn Away** or **Turn Against**. Both are equally damaging to the relationship. Turning Away generally ignores the Bid. It can be a literal Turning Away, like rolling over in the bed, or it can be symbolic, by disappearing into the newspaper or, more likely, the nearest screen. Turning Against is much more violent. We can turn against by mocking the Bid or by punishing the Bidder. "*What do you want? Can't you see I'm right in the middle of something!*" Both are equally damaging. The difference is that Turning Against leads into Conflict, while Turning Away leads to **Disengagement**.

Turning Toward leads to more Turning Toward. It's a positive feedback cycle.

So get good at Turning Toward. It takes practice, but the good news is the research shows that Turning Toward leads to more Turning Toward. It's a positive feedback cycle. And in practice, there's really no difference between Turning Toward and Enthusiastically Turning Toward. That means, you don't have to say, "*You betcha! You look amazing! I love passing the guacamole! Let's get busy with the sexytime!*" You simply have to be attuned to your partner's bids and respond with kind awareness.

I have to confess, I'm not great at Turning Toward. Or at least I wasn't until I started practicing. At first, I just committed to hearing the sound of my wife's voice. Not listening, just hearing. Once I heard the sounds, I would realize I needed to pay attention. Then I'd literally take a few seconds (or more) to remember the sounds I heard and reassemble them in my brain so that I could actually understand them. Finally, I'd formulate a response, any response, that indicated that I was interested in loving my wife.

You've surely learned by now that my brain works in

odd ways, but the point is that it works for me. Feel free to start anywhere. Again, you don't have to have a complete strategy mapped out. Turning Toward fuels Turning Toward, keeping you solidly on the left side of the picture so you can spend a lot more time in the realm of stability and intimacy. To be sure, sometimes you have to go through Conflict to get there. But you can save yourself a lot of grief by building up the kind of positive sentiment that leads to overall relationship satisfaction.

Turning Discussion Questions:

1. Think of some recent Bids you made to your partner. What was the response? How did it make you feel?
2. Turning Away leads to disengagement, while Turning Against leads to conflict. Why do you think both are equally damaging?
3. Do you think Turning Toward means that you must always *accept* your partner's Bid? How could you say no but still Turn Toward them?
4. Think about a time you have Turned Away or Against. What happened? What might it have looked like to Turn Toward instead?
5. Discuss with your partner what it would look like to Turn Toward each other more consistently. How might you need to change your listening habits? Do you need to change how you communicate your bids? Commit to practicing this week.

U

U is for Understanding

There are maybe a half-dozen sound bites that frame Gottman Method Couples Therapy. One is *Small Things Often*. Small Things Often is the idea that it's the small positive things done often that make the difference in relationships that thrive. Small things add up and create a surplus of good-will and affection, making it easy to handle some of the many mundane trials that couples face every day. Another sound bite, *Process Is Everything*, means that how you talk through those mundane trials matters more than whether you solve them. Ultimately, your relationship is more important than the issue.

A third sound bite, and one of my favorites, is *Understanding Must Precede Advice*. This, of course, rings of ancient wisdom that could have come from Buddha or Gandhi. More recently, it's entered popular consciousness in the form of Steven Covey's 5th Habit for Highly Effective People: *Seek first to understand, then to be understood*. Even more recently, filmmaker Jason Headley has created a short video wherein a woman complains to her husband about dealing with overwhelming pressure, poor sleep, and multiple snagged sweaters. When he points out that she has a nail sticking out of her forehead, she snaps, "Stop trying to fix it. It's not about the nail!"[1]

In practice, *Understanding Must Precede Advice* is difficult. This is partly because we want so desperately to be understood. We're actually wired that way. I recently read about a sculpture dating back approximately 13,000 years, of two reindeer carved into a mammoth tusk. As the sculpture is beautifully detailed but appears to have no practical purpose, historians have classified it as one of the earliest known expressions of art, and cited it as evidence that humans have an innate desire to make their inner world known. The impulse to communicate our opinions and ideas, and to be understood, is at the very least deeply ingrained. And it's hard to suppress what is, essentially, our humanity.

The impulse to communicate our opinions and ideas, and to be understood, is at the very least deeply ingrained.

The second reason that *Understanding Must Precede Advice* is so hard is that it's quite easy, and comforting, to give advice. The video I referenced earlier ("It's Not About the Nail"—look it up!) is funny because it's true. I love

1. Jason Headley, "It's Not About the Nail," http://www.jasonheadley.com, (October 15, 2014).

solving problems, and if I'm honest, I'd rather solve your problems than my own. After all, if I can fix you, then I get to feel good about myself without even having to look at my own stuff. Win win! It's a trait especially common among men, but plenty of women struggle with it as well. And no matter your gender, it's a particular challenge for a therapist. I am convinced, however, that we serve our partners (and our clients) better when we avoid the temptation to give advice and instead offer understanding. But again, it's far from easy. So how do we avoid the trap?

Think of a cue ball. You probably know exactly what it looks like—you can even imagine the weight. No surprises there, right? I once read, however, that relative to the surface of the earth, the ridges and valleys on a cue ball are higher than the highest mountains and deeper than the deepest oceans on our planet. I think that's kind of wild. Now imagine a conversation (or a conflict) where the topic is a cue ball tossed back and forth. All too often, we fail to consider what is actually being said, largely because we think we already know. We see a familiar surface and fail to look much beyond that, if at all. That cue ball isn't really all that interesting, and it's certainly not as interesting as the thing I want to say, so I'm going to toss it back without even looking at it.

But consider if that cue ball was a globe. Bear with me for a moment. Imagine the conversation is a detailed desktop globe heaved back and forth. Much more interesting, isn't it? Have you ever noticed how much bigger the Pacific Ocean is than the Atlantic? Do you know close

Alaska and Russia are? How far do the Rocky Mountains run north to south? Which is bigger, Germany or Peru? You have to look. You have to pay attention and compare and ask questions. You've got to look at that globe from different angles. It's not as quick or apparently clear as the cue ball conversation so it's easier to pay attention and you'll probably learn something.

Understanding means taking a second look even, and especially, when you think you've heard it all before.

Now remember that the cue ball you had before may actually be more textured than the detailed, 3-D you're holding. It, too, is nuanced and surprising, only you can't see it at first glance. You have to look closely. You might need a microscope. But in order to appreciate the complexity, you've got to entertain the possibility that you don't have complete clarity about the situation, the conversation, the complication. Understanding means taking a second look even, and especially, when you think you've heard it all before.

Understanding requires looking, considering, examining, comparing, and contrasting. It requires more curiosity than certainty, and more safety than solution. It requires humility. And it can feel counterintuitive. However, as you build trust and intimacy through "Small Things Often" and "Process is Everything," you'll find you can more confidently practice "Understanding Must

Precede Advice." The first step is to set aside the impulse to express yourself and your temptation to solve. Once you've done that, you've got a much better chance of discovering what that cue ball, or globe, or conversation, or conflict is really about. Because most likely, it's not about the nail.

Understanding Discussion Questions:

1. Think about a time when you received advice without understanding. How did you feel? Did you want advice?
2. Consider a recent conflict. How was understanding offered? What about advice? How was each received?
3. When your partner comes to you with a problem, is your impulse to offer solutions or understanding? Why do you think that is? How does this impulse affect conflict management in your relationship?
4. Why might "Small Things Often" and "Process is Everything" set you up well for "Understanding Must Precede Advice"?
5. What are some cue-ball issues in your relationship? What might be the hidden ridges and valleys (or fears and dreams) hidden beneath a familiar exterior?

V

V is for Violence

I'm writing this chapter in October, which is Domestic Violence Awareness month. I appreciate that we as a country have devoted a month to such an important issue, although unfortunately I think it's something we're already quite aware of these days, even without the reminder. At the moment, there's a powerful ad campaign for a non-profit called "No More," wherein television personalities and NFL players call for a stop to domestic violence. The ad features football players largely because multiple stories have recently surfaced about prominent athletes (in the NFL and beyond) accused and/or convicted of domestic violence. If you're a therapist, you've heard such stories in your office more often than you'd care to admit, and not just in October. Even if you're not paying attention, you must know that domestic violence awareness isn't important simply because the media says so.

It's a tough topic. Not for the faint of heart. And I fear that, due to word-count constraints, I won't be able to bring the proper gravitas to the experiences of the *one in three* American women who are abused each year. In the time it takes me to write this sentence, another woman will be assaulted or beaten in the US. Just typing those words makes me feel powerless, but not nearly as powerless as the 1.3 million women who will be assaulted by a partner this year.

The observant reader will note that I haven't even scratched the surface with regard to violence perpetrated against women and children worldwide. You might also be inclined to remind me that 85 percent of adult domestic violence victims are women. I could, and maybe I should, dedicate 15 percent of my word count to the very real plight of abused men. But the point is that these statistics—these stories—are tragic. And perhaps we're not as powerless as we think.

As a therapist, I find the question of how to assess violence a tricky one. Research suggests that half of all couples seeking therapy have experienced violence in their relationship, whether they tell you or not. In some cases, when there's violence in the relationship, therapy can do more harm than good. In any case, it is important to distinguish between violence and battery. Dr. Anne Ganley defines battery as follows:

> *Battery is a form of abuse where the primary aggressor employs violence ranging from pushing to relationship rape to homicide, to enhance the aggressor's control over their partner, leading the partner to modify their behaviors in daily life. It is*

meant to instill fear and intimidation.[1]

When battery is present, couples therapy is inappropriate. Identify and provide appropriate referrals for your client(s). Battery is evidence of what Dr. Gottman calls **Characterological Violence**, where one partner clearly demonstrates controlling and dominating behavior. In this case, your client is in clear and immediate danger, and you have a responsibility to refer him or her to a treatment center, hotline, shelter, specialist, or the police. If you suspect battery is present but one or both partners are denying it, refer. If you're not sure, refer. It's irresponsible, unethical, and likely even illegal for you to begin couples therapy when Characterological Violence is present.

But what about when violence is more subtle—what Dr. Gottman calls **Situational Violence**? Situational violence occurs most often with couples who lack conflict resolution skills. Generally both partners feel remorse, understand the impact, and internalize the blame. In this case, treatment for the couple prioritizes conflict management, with an emphasis on flooding and repair. The couple must also learn to recognize and rein in the Four Horsemen so that conflict does not escalate. Eventually the therapist should help the couple replace toxic conflict patterns with a deeper sense of friendship and shared meaning. I have intentionally not gone into detail

1. Anne Ganley, Treating Men Who Batter: Theory, Practice, and Programs, ed. P. Lynn Caesar and L. Kevin Hamberger, (New York: Springer Publishing Company, 1989).

here because my goal is not to train therapists as much as to raise awareness. Also, therapists aren't necessarily my audience just now. If you are a therapist and do want to talk about this, my contact information is at the end of this book. Please reach out to me.

Situational violence occurs most often with couples who lack conflict resolution skills.

Many of you reading this are wondering what to do about your own relationship. You may be wondering if there's hope or help. There is. No doubt your community has resources available to you, and you can also contact the National Domestic Violence Hotline (1-800-799-7233, 1-800-787-3224 (TTY), or visit thehotline.org). You may be wondering if what you're experiencing is Characterological or Situational Violence. If you're not sure, I suspect it's more severe. It may not make a difference. Domestic violence is never the victim's fault. Seek help.

If you're certain that you and your partner are simply bad at conflict, then get better at it. Remember that you are adults. You have a responsibility to behave like adults. When conflict escalates in your relationship:

- **Self-Soothe When Flooded:** This is the first step to conflict regulation. "Flooding," in the Gottman lexicon, refers to that feeling of being completely emotionally overwhelmed during a conflict. It often comes with physical indicators. Do you feel shaky or lightheaded? Is your pulse racing, like 95 beats per minute or higher? If so, take a break. Try 10-15 deep breaths. Go for a walk. You simply cannot engage your partner in a meaningful way when you are flooded, so give yourself time to calm down.

- **Identify your Common Enemy:** Situational Violence occurs when partners identify one another as the enemy. This is a bad strategy. You need to define your *common* enemy—in this case, it could be the violence itself. When negativity rises up, remember you have a responsibility (and literally, response-ability) to deny it access to your relationship. Identifying a common enemy helps you become more attuned to each other's needs so that you can fight with, not against, one another.
- **Practice Repair:** You may recall that Repair is any statement or action—silly or otherwise—that prevents negativity from escalating out of control. It's an advanced skill for couples, but skills can be learned. You've heard the phrase, "practice makes perfect"? I actually disagree. Practice makes *permanent*. If you practice poor conflict management, it'll become permanent. Practicing repair shifts the balance away from the conflict and toward the couple. Get creative.

Whether you are a therapist or a client, a victim or an abuser, a running back or a goalkeeper, you can do something about domestic violence. It's a solvable problem. It begins with awareness (thanks October) but it requires attention and action. Pay attention. Act. Ask for help. Respond.

You are not powerless.

Violence Discussion Questions:

1. How might characterological violence look different from situational violence?
2. Do you agree that situational violence can respond to therapy, while characterological violence requires immediate removal from the situation? Why or why not?
3. Can you remember a time you felt "flooded" during a conflict? How did you respond? What was the result?
4. If situational violence exists in your relationship, what techniques can you implement today to work toward better conflict resolution? If violence does not exist in your relationship, what skills can you sharpen to ensure it stays that way? (In either case, it may be helpful to reread "R is for Repair.")
5. Think about a recent conflict you had with your partner. What do you think was the "common enemy" in that particular case? Did you identify it during the conflict? Why or why not?

W is for Wednesday

What would you guess is the most common reason couples come into therapy? The lady who cuts my hair thinks it's "affairs." My neighbor thinks it's "empty nest syndrome." What do you think?

Couples come into my practice for any number of reasons. Often enough, it's conflict over finances or in-laws or work-life balance. Sometimes, it's anticipation of the transition into marriage, followed soon thereafter by managing the transition to parenthood. I suppose the thing I hear most often is, "we're having trouble communicating," but personally, I think that's a cop-out. Not that communication can't be an issue, but "trouble with communication" has become something of a catch-all phrase that doesn't really mean anything specific. I once had a deaf client who was having "communication issues" with her boyfriend. Their issues had nothing to do with her disability—they simply didn't know how to talk to one another. He once said, without an ounce of irony, "I have no idea why she can't hear me." Their issues were far more complex than their presenting problem. They usually are.

If there are "Seven Principles for Making Marriage Work", as Dr. John Gottman suggests, there are dozens of reasons why marriages fail. Of course there are the Four Horsemen of the Apocalypse, affairs, work stress, family conflicts, and money issues. There are any number of huge challenges that couples all around you are struggling with. But my personal belief is that the main reason couples are struggling is Wednesday.

You thought W was for Weddings, didn't you? As I'm writing this, wedding chatter is especially loud, likely due to a recent study linking the cost of one's wedding to the likelihood for a happy marriage. (The short version: have more than 200 people and spend less than $1,000.) There's no shortage of information on weddings. But as important as that one day is, it's not nearly as important as Wednesday.

Wednesday is the day that you either make a deposit into or withdrawal from the emotional bank account of your relationship.

Wednesday is the day you make or break a marriage. Wednesday—the normal, mundane today—is the day you can choose to learn a little more about your partner. Wednesday is the day you turn toward or away from their bids for affection or attention or approval. Wednesday is the day that you either make a deposit into or withdrawal from the emotional bank account of your relationship. Wednesday is the day you decide to prioritize understanding over advice.

Dr. Gottman's research suggests that the average couple waits six years before seeking help for relationship problems. That's over *300 Wednesdays* of unhappiness. And keep in mind, half of all failed marriages end in the first seven years. All of this means the average couple lives with unhappiness for far too long. I wonder why. I mean, I actually wonder, out loud, to my clients: Why?

The truth is, no one ever woke up one day and said, "Wow, my marriage is suddenly not as good as I'd hoped, but I refuse to seek help." It creeps up on you, because you're not paying attention. Instead, you're paying attention to things that are louder, more urgent, more essential, and frankly, things that are easier. Your marriage becomes a completed task, checked off the list and forgotten in order to make room for everything else. As such, too many couples allow themselves to settle into a daily routine that doesn't look anything like the relationship they committed to on their wedding day. But it's easier to just keep doing what they're doing and assume it will get better tomorrow, or next week, or eventually. Left to itself, it probably won't. It's hard work to steward a marriage every day, but it's the most important work you can do.

So how do you start? Take Wednesday—take today—and make a choice. Choose to reach out to your partner in specific, intentional ways. A loving note. A profound question. Do the dishes even if it's not your day. When I told a friend what I was writing about for W, he slyly noted that Wednesday was also "hump day," making sure the euphemism wasn't lost on me (it wasn't). Indeed, make Wednesday the day you choose to pursue intimacy with your partner. Maybe today is the day that you re-connect through sex. Or through a different kind of sex. Try a new room or time of day. Take longer or not as long. If sex is not possible or practical, maybe squeeze in a six-second kiss or cuddle a little longer. Or try sleeping naked for a change.

Too many couples allow themselves to settle into a daily routine that doesn't look anything like the relationship they committed to on their wedding day.

Whatever you do, do it on purpose. *Today* is the day you protect your relationship from an affair. *Today* is the day you solve that nagging solvable problem. *Today* is the day that you turn toward your partner a little more and a little more intentionally. *Today* is the day that you work on "communication issues." Your relationship is bigger than your presenting problems. Take care of Wednesday. I promise you it's even more important than your wedding day.

Wednesday Discussion Questions:

1. What have you believed is the primary reason for marital problems? How do you think that's related to the issue of "Wednesday"?

2. Why do you think so many couples wait six years before seeking help for problems in their relationship?

3. Are there things in your day to day life that often take priority over stewarding your marriage? When was the last time you sacrificed a daily task for your relationship?

4. Think about a time your partner surprised you by making a "Wednesday" special or important. How did that make you feel? How did your partner feel?

5. What are some things in your relationship that often get glossed over, delayed, or that are simply never addressed? Can you address one of those things today? How might that one thing strengthen your relationship?

X

X is for X-Rated

My first exposure to pornography was over 30 years ago. It was in the basement of my childhood home, where my dad had poorly hidden a dusty stack of *Playboy* magazines. I remember thinking that, as long as I left the correct one on the top, he'd never know I'd spent an afternoon flipping through the pages (turns out this was not a good strategy). Many years later, I remember finding a folded up page from a more x-rated magazine in a bathroom of a mall restaurant. For a teenage boy in the pre-internet age, this was an Indiana Jones caliber find. I can still recall the thrill of that secret treasure.

Three decades later, access to pornography is far easier. Pornographers are savvy marketers who have been engaged for years in a relentless pursuit to make porn mainstream, and they're winning. Internet porn is practically unavoidable—anyone with a smartphone can view it at a moment's notice. Every second of every day, roughly 30,000 internet users are viewing pornography. Twelve percent of all websites and 25 percent of all search engine requests are related to pornography.

In 2013, porn sites got more visitors per month than Netflix, Amazon, and Twitter combined.[1] Even if you don't seek it out, chances are your e-mail spam folder is packed with graphic offers and propositions. It's a far cry from crumpled pages of erotica hiding in the darkest corners of our everyday world.

Let me just say, as a therapist, that I have no moral objection to the use of pornography. I do believe—both personally and professionally—that an unexamined relationship with pornography *always* does more harm than good.

The most devastating effects of porn use are more emotional than physical, and more relational than personal.

Scientists have been exploring the effects of porn on the body for years, wondering about its impact on everything from brain chemistry and libido to mental health issues like anxiety, depression, and motivation. The general consensus is that it's not good. But porn affects more than just the body. Dr. Gottman's own scientific research revealed that masturbating to pornographic images results in the secretion of oxytocin and vasopressin, hormones linked to attachment and emotional connection. This discovery points to perhaps the most

1. The Huffington Post, "Porn Sites Get More Visitors Each Month Than Netflix, Amazon and Twitter Combined," http://huffingtonpost.com, (May 4, 2013).

significant factor of porn use: its impact on personal relationships.

In *What Makes Love Last?*, Dr. Gottman unambiguously weighs in on the issue, noting that "even non-compulsive use of [pornographic] images can damage a committed relationship." He expands his argument by explaining, "most porn encourages steps that can lead to betrayal," including the loss of emotional connection, secret keeping, negative comparisons, and dismissing the partner as unattractive and, even worse, unworthy. The implication is clear: The most devastating effects of porn use are more emotional than physical, and more relational than personal. One of my clients, struggling with pornography addiction, has even called it "soul destroying."

My goal here is not to climb up on a soapbox. Instead, it's to offer a sobering perspective on what is becoming a mainstream "reality" based almost entirely in myth. I've compiled four damaging myths about pornography for you to consider.

Myth of Perfection: Most pornography is based on the idea of physical and sexual perfection. The women in mainstream pornography have stereotypically ideal proportions and they are mostly free of the blemishes, wrinkles, and love handles that are common to most of the women you know. The men in porn industry are marathon lovers with six-pack abs and perfect hair. The sex itself usually involves multiple orgasms for her and always an orgasm for him—one that his partner is more than happy to provide at all costs. None of the participants ever sneeze or burp or fart. The sex is never awkward or uncomfortable (unless by design). It's perfect. He's perfect. She's perfect. And it's a lie.

Myth of Ease: One of the most tragic myths of pornography is that sex is easy. Pornographic sex exists in a world without needy children or ringing phones or football games that will be over in just ten minutes. Sex is never postponed by fatigue or illness. It is never rejected. Initiation is a simple process. Foreplay is quick and painless, if not skipped altogether. It's a world where you can sleep with the a cheerleader, a plumber, a teacher, a pizza delivery guy, and a police officer without discretion or consequence. There is no fear of rejection and no resistance of initiation. It's easy. And it's a lie.

Myth of Escape: I often hear clients describe their use of pornography as an escape from the norm. A way "to spice it up a bit" or "to get some relief from the mundane." But this narrow view clouds the reality that a temporary escape from the real world can actually lead into a more permanent and less healthy attachment. The typical narrative of pornography is pretty simple: strangers meet, have sex, and never see each other again. Even within that pattern there are consistent sub-patterns that are relatively standardized and predictable (and, in fact, mundane). Problems arise when porn users become more attached to that pattern than to the person with whom they're committed to having sex. That attachment bonds the user to a fetish of impersonal sex, ultimately leading them away from personal relationships and back into pornography. This can lead to overuse and compulsion. It feels like escape. And it's a lie.

Myth of Privacy: Many users justify their porn use as no big deal because it doesn't affect anybody else. This is naive. In addition to the myths discussed above—all of which have serious implications for others—consider the simple notion that porn use is a gateway to sexual escalation. Dr. Gottman has articulated a "typical" descent from porn to infidelity simply by seeking out increasing stimulation. Eventually, private online activity leads to personal interactions and giving yourself permission to cross boundaries you swore you'd never cross. Once this happens, you compromise your own privacy as well as the privacy of your family and community. Privacy is a lovely idea. And it's a lie.

Problems arise when porn users become more attached to that pattern than to the person with whom they're committed to having sex.

I should go on record to say that porn use doesn't *always* negatively impact personal relationships. Dr. Gottman notes that "betrayal is not a concern if the couple uses porn to enhance their mutual desire and pleasure during lovemaking." But this type of use is, of course, the exception rather than the rule. Most porn use is done in secret, and "the secret itself creates distance and diminishes intimacy, which may in turn increase the use of porn," according to Dr. Gottman. In cases when partners use porn together, the key is, as always, agreement and intention. Without that, the most likely scenario is that pornography is being used to turn away from your partner and toward a fantasy.

Earlier, I used the phrase "unexamined relationship" in reference to pornography. I used that phrase on purpose because I've found that it can be helpful to personify things in order to articulate the role they play. I've had a relationship with porn for a long time. There have been times when we spent a lot of time together. We've also gone months and even years without hanging out at all. Ultimately, we've drifted apart—primarily because I realized it didn't make sense for me to hang out with someone who lied to me all the time. What does your relationship look like?

If a relationship with porn is undermining your relationships, I encourage you to take steps toward repair. Take a close look at the story of your relationship with porn and your sexual story in general. If you're not ready to do this with your partner, consider talking with a professional or a friend, or spend some time with your journal. In any case, it's important to undertake an honest examination to make sure you're seeking intimacy and truth rather than settling for myths.

Fun Fact: During the course of my research for this piece, I learned that the least popular day for Americans to view porn is Thanksgiving Day. I wonder if that tells us something about the relationship between gratitude and intimacy. Perhaps it should.

X-Rated Discussion Questions:

1. What are your feelings about the use of pornography in a committed relationship? How does your partner feel about it?
2. Has pornography played a role in your current or past relationships? How do you feel it has impacted those relationships?
3. What myth or myths of pornography do you find most enticing? Why do you think that is?
4. Gottman argues that keeping porn use a secret can lead to diminished intimacy and can severely damage a relationship. Do you think this is true only for pornography or for secrets in general? Why?
5. Examine your relationship with porn, and with sex in general. What decisions have you made along the way? What, if anything, would you like to change now? With whom are you comfortable sharing your story?

Y

Y is for Yes

Most relationships start with Yes. *Can I buy you a drink? Would you like to go out sometime? May I kiss you?* Yes.

Do you remember your first Yes-es? Do you remember the thrill of connecting to another person? The joy of getting to know one another? Do you remember the world that began opening up on the strength of that tiny word? Do you remember how that answer led to more questions? Yes does more than answer a question. It creates opportunity and invites possibility. Yes allows for a kind of mathematical magic, multiplying itself as you continue to use it. It's a powerful word. Author and psychiatrist Dr. Dan Siegel draws attention to this power with this pretty simple exercise:

Notice how you feel when you read these words:

No.
No.
No.
No.
No.
No.

Now sense how you feel when you read these words:

Yes.

Yes.

Yes.

Yes.

Yes.

Yes.

What did you notice?

Seriously, pause for just a moment and notice what you noticed. I was surprisingly moved when I first did the exercise earlier this year. With "no," I felt scolded and alone. I even started breathing heavy. With "yes," I felt relaxed and relieved. Just now, I did it again with a video of Dr. Siegel performing the exercise during a lecture, and I had an almost identical experience.

Thriving relationships exist only when both partners are consistently saying Yes.

Dr. Siegel suggests that "yes" makes us more receptive and that "when we are receptive, presence can be created. Practicing presence is essential for the thriving of our relationships."[1] I'd also argue that thriving relationships exist only when both partners are consistently saying Yes. John Gottman's model of thriving relationships, called the Sound Relationship House, is supported

1. Dr. Dan Siegel, http://www.facebook.com, (July 2, 2013).

by the twin pillars of trust and commitment. Trust is established as partners ask the question, "*Can I count on you?*" and then answer "*Yes*" with both conviction and consistency. Commitment is built by reinforcing that "Yes" over time, even through conflict and mis-communication and job stress and empty nests and few too many drinks and a few extra pounds.

But it's not just the walls of the house that are dependent upon Yes. Yes is present throughout the entire structure. Imagine your house. Imagine that every room, every closet, lamp, couch, utensil, every corner—even the dusty one—is asking you a question about your relationship. At the foundational level, those questions are about the relational friendship. Do you know your partner's story? Do you like your partner? Do you tell him? Are you attracted to your partner? Are you proud of her? Are you grateful? Do you say so? An abundance of Yes leads to Gottman's "Positive Perspective," a level of the Sound Relationship House that is essential for thriving relationships. When the relationship has a surplus of positive energy, partners are better equipped to face the harder questions that inevitably come up.

Psychologist Dan Wile says, "When choosing a long-term partner... you will inevitably be choosing a particular set of unsolvable problems."[1] This is just to say all relationships have conflict. The middle level of the Sound Relationship House asks couples to manage that conflict with Yes: *Yes, I will seek to understand your problem*

---

2. Daniel B. Wile, "My Quotes," http://danwile.com, (December 9, 2014).

before I seek to solve it. Yes, I will work to cultivate empathy for your point of view. Yes, I will respect your dream. Yes, I will dialogue with you, even—and especially—when I disagree with you. Yes, I will remember to talk with you like you are someone I love. Relationships that handle conflict well do not always agree, but they make sure to answer the important questions with Yes.

The truth is, most negotiations break down because parties remain focused on their differences.

A critical skill in conflict management is the art of compromise. If you pay any attention to politics or meetings at work or any number of self-help books, you've likely heard that word a zillion times—or at least enough that it's lost a bit of it's power. The truth is, most negotiations break down because parties remain focused on their differences. They concentrate solely on protecting their territory. The Gottmans suggest switching the focus toward identifying what you have in common, then articulating and pursuing the common goal. They call it "Getting to Yes."

The attic of the Sound Relationship House is about creating shared meaning and making life dreams come true. In order to do that, you have to say Yes to each other. Will you dream with me? Will you create with me? Can we do something that's never been done before? Yes opens doors to ideas and opportunities that you may not have considered. You don't have to go skydiving or spelunking, but you could. You could also just start at home. Start by asking your partner what their dreams are. Do you know? If not, turn that "no" into a "yes" as soon as possible. It's hard to pursue dreams together if you don't know what they are.

Look for opportunities for Yes in your house. Look in every corner, even the dusty ones. You may have to pay a little extra attention. You may have to be a little more present. I promise you, your partner is asking you questions all the time, even if you can't hear them. Saying Yes is a great way to start being present and create a thriving relationship.

Yes Discussion Questions:

1. What are some of the first "Yes"es in your relationship? What are some "No"s that stand out? How do you feel remembering each?
2. What are some ways you and your partner say Yes to each other in your day to day life? What are some ways you say No?
3. Do you agree that thriving relationships exist only when couples consistently say Yes to each other? Why or why not? What would "consistently saying yes" look like in your relationship?
4. Think about a recent conflict between you and your partner. How did you say Yes and/or No to each other? Did you reach a compromise? If so, how? If not, what could have helped you find common ground?
5. Discuss dreams with your partner. What are some dreams you need to say Yes to? What dreams do you need your partner to hear? How might saying Yes to each other's dreams impact your relationship house?

Z

Z is for Zed

Here we are at Z—or Zed for my Canadian friends—signaling the end of the alphabet. I was tempted to write Z is for Zach, and tell you all about my experience working through these twenty-six topics, but I'm not that much of a narcissist. Instead, I'll turn my attention toward two of my favorite concepts in the Gottman lexicon. Lucky for me they both start with Z.

The first is the **Zeigarnik Effect** named for Bluma Zeigarnik, a Lithuanian psychologist who is credited with a specific insight regarding memory. As the story goes, she was observing waiters in a cafe and became curious about how they remembered customer orders. She noted that these waiters were able to remember even the most complicated orders in detail until the moment they submitted the order to the kitchen.

Her speculation, later confirmed, was that people remember uncompleted or interrupted tasks better than completed tasks. This notion has implications for both hard-working students and couch potatoes. We tune in to *Scandal* week after week because our mind wants to close the loop on the latest cliffhanger. When students take breaks from studying to perform other tasks, they remember the material better than if they'd crammed for hours with no breaks. Even procrastinators (like me) can benefit by simply starting an activity, because the Zeigarnik Effect suggests that the brain will then continue noodling on the task until it is completed.

When arguments or disappointing events go unaddressed, it becomes a painful memory that lives on "like a stone in one's shoe."

Dr. Gottman has applied the Ziegarnik Effect to relationships, noting that when arguments or disappointing events go unaddressed, it becomes a painful memory that lives on "like a stone in one's shoe." It's a constant, nagging reminder of unfinished business that can lead to negative sentiment toward the partner and the relationship. Ultimately the memory claims more power than it deserves. Dr. Gottman again: "Between lovers, arguments that end with confessions, amends, and deeper understanding of one another tend to be soon forgotten, although their legacy is a stronger, more enduring relationship." It seems clear that couples need to learn to process issues together as they arise. And while these days I'm less and less convinced that a negative memory can ever truly be erased, I do believe that it can be replaced by a stronger, more positive experience of empathy and understanding. That's where the magic is.

Unfortunately, most couples aren't terribly skilled at this process. The truth is that most *people* aren't terribly skilled at this process. We're really good at stating our case, defending our position, and protecting our turf. On the flip side, we're also pretty good at avoiding conflict altogether. It's a dichotomy commonly known as the "fight or flight" response, and it's actually the way we're wired. But this particular wiring doesn't often serve our relationships well. In fact, it leads us into today's second "Z" topic: the **zero-sum game**.

In game theory, the zero-sum game is the idea that in any interaction, one party's gain is precisely balanced by another party's loss. When I win, you lose. Obviously this doesn't work in a relationship. In fact, I'm convinced that whenever one person wins at the expense of another—especially in a marriage—then both partners lose.

I'm convinced that whenever one person wins at the expense of another—especially in a marriage—then both partners lose.

Couples can break the zero-sum game pattern by emphasizing (once again) empathy and understanding, but it requires work to ensure that the relationship wins. This means that even when you're in disagreement, you're still considering your partner's best interests. This isn't easy, but it is a skill. Which means, you *can* learn it. Start by changing the way you think about the "game" of your relationship. The zero-sum game is a finite game, designed to be won. Relationships are a different kind of game, designed to be prolonged and enjoyed. Read more on this in "R is for Repair."

The good news is that you can combat the impact of the Zeigarnik Effect and of zero-sum mentality in your relationship. But you must make *process* a priority. Process means dealing with the stones in your shoes as soon as possible, through intimate conversation and attunement. It means getting to know your partner's story and their perspective almost better than your own. It means learning new skills. And believing in magic. Your relationship is worth the effort. And so are you.

Zed Discussion Questions:

1. Can you think of a time when you experienced the Zeigarnik Effect to your benefit? What about a time it seemed to hurt you or your relationship?
2. Why is it important to deal with "stone in your shoe" issues sooner rather than later?
3. When confronted with conflict, do you tend to gravitate toward "fight" or "flight"?
4. Are there times in your relationship when you feel you and your partner played a zero-sum game? How do you feel about those issues today?
5. Think about a past "stone in the shoe" issue. What stopped you from processing it fully? If it's been resolved, how did you come to a resolution? If it hasn't been resolved, how can you engage empathy and understanding to continue your process?

The Sound Relationship House (SRH)

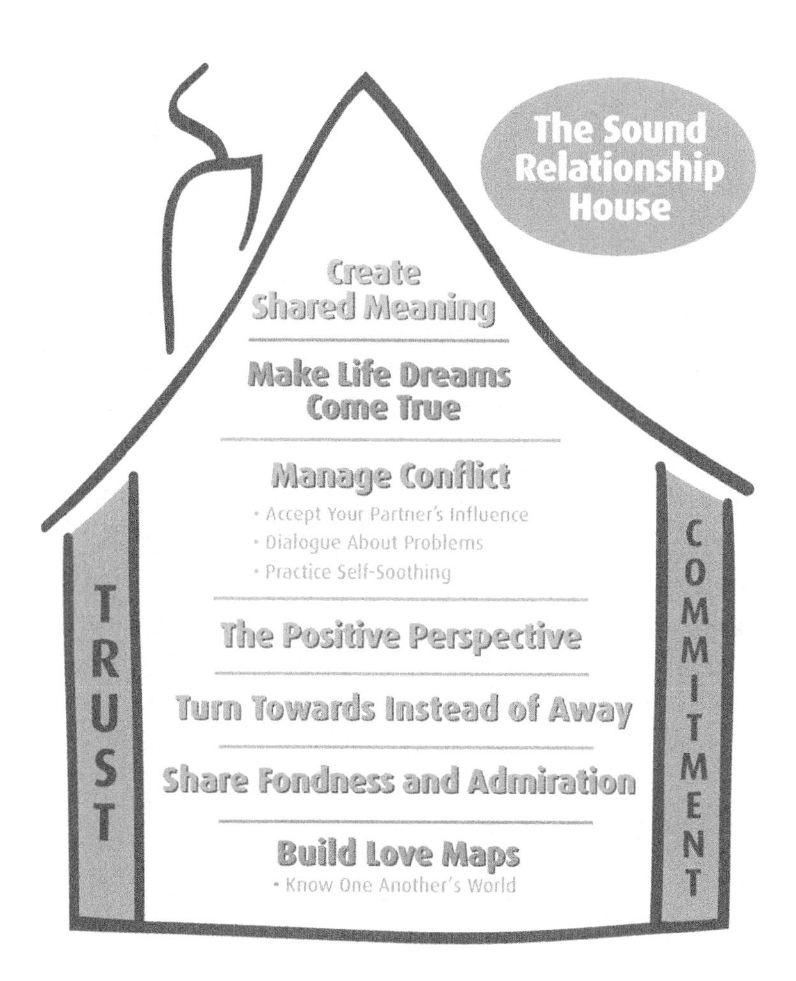

Learn more in Dr. John Gottman's bestselling book,
The Seven Principles for Making Marriage Work.

About the Author

Zach Brittle has been teaching, coaching, and counseling couples for over 15 years. He is a Certified Gottman Therapist with a private practice in evidence-based couples therapy. He is also the founder of and teacher at **forBetter** which offers online resources for couples. Zach and his wife have been happily married for 19 out of 20 years. They live in Seattle, WA with their two very cool daughters. They own a mini-van and most of the silverware they got as wedding presents.

Go to forBetter.us and use the code MIM-ABC for $100 off the online course MARRIAGE in MOTION.

About The Gottman Institute

Co-founded by Drs. John and Julie Gottman in 1996, The Gottman Institute is an internationally-renowned organization dedicated to combining wisdom from research and practice to support and strengthen marriages and relationships by offering workshops and resources for couples, families, and professionals.

Recommended Reading

Completely revised and updated, Dr. John Gottman's *New York Times* bestseller, *The Seven Principles for Making Marriage Work*. Now over a million copies sold, this book remains the definitive guide for anyone who wants their relationship to attain its highest potential.

Workshops for Couples

The Art & Science of Love weekend workshop for couples is designed to strengthen relationships through engaging presentations and experiential activities. Presented by Drs. John and Julie Gottman in Seattle, WA five times per year, this two-day workshop will give you new insights and research-based skills that can dramatically improve the intimacy and friendship in your relationship and help you manage conflict in a healthy, positive way. Learn more at gottman.com.

The Gottman Institute

Researching and Restoring Relationships

The Gottman Institute
2101 4th Ave. Suite 1750
Seattle, WA 98121

Phone: (888) 523-9042
Fax: (206) 523-7306

Website: www.gottman.com
Blog: www.gottmanblog.com
Facebook: /GottmanInstitute
Instagram: @gottmaninstitute
Twitter: @GottmanInst
Pinterest: /GottmanInst

39500680R00099

Made in the USA
Middletown, DE
17 March 2019